Also by John Ashbery

Poetry

Fiction

Plays

Criticism

Can

You

Hear,

Bird

CAN YOU HEAR, BIRD

poems

JOHN ASHBERY

Farrar, Straus and Giroux

New York

Library of Congress Cataloging-in-Publication Data
Ashbery, John.
    Can you hear, bird / by John Ashbery.
        p. cm.
    I. Title.
PS3501.S475C36 1995   811'.54—dc20   95-288 CIP

*The author gratefully acknowledges the following publications in
which poems in* Can You Hear, Bird *first appeared:* American
Poetry Review, Antaeus, Arshile, Chelsea, The Colorado Review,
Cover, Epoch, Grand Street, The Harvard Review, *Kaldewey
Press*, The New Yorker, 1995 Biennial Exhibition Catalog
(Whitney Museum), PN Review, The Paris Review, Poetry
(Chicago), Privates, Times Literary Supplement, Writing for
Bernadette *(Great Barrington, MA; The Figures, 1995)*, The Yale
Review, Denver Quarterly, London Quarterly, The London
Review of Books, *and* The New Republic.

for

Harry Mathews

and

Marie Chaix

Contents

Can

You

Hear,

Bird

A Day at the Gate

A loose and dispiriting
wind took over from the grinding of traffic.
Clouds from the distillery
blotted out the sky. Ocarina sales plummeted.

Believe you me it was a situation
Aladdin's lamp might have ameliorated. And where was I?
Among architecture, magazines, recycled fish,
waiting for the wear and tear
to show up on my chart. Good luck,

bonne chance. Remember me to the zithers
and their friends, the ondes martenot.
Only I say: What comes this way withers
automatically. And the fog, drastically.

As one mercurial teardrop glozes
an empire's classified documents, so
other softnesses decline the angles
of the waiting. Tall, pissed-off,
dressed in this day's clothes,
holding its umbrella, he half turned away
with a shooshing sound. Said he needed us.
Said the sky shall be kelly green tonight.

A New Octagon

Over a cup of flaming tea, the ogre assessed
my chances. Nothing in this blue vault belongs
where you put it; therefore are you the dupe
of its nonchalance. Try to wriggle free, remembering

what the great collector said: Serenity is a mild bridle
lending dignity to any occasion. The best truss
is the severest, but your village
ends where mine begins. Angry little houses litigate;

the roof leaks. Present your wrist for stamping
as you go out into the northwestern territories, otherwise
we'll see whose absence becomes it.
Daughters Tiffany and Brittany concurred. There

isn't much in the way of agony impeding the astral
path you seek. On with the
ways and
the variance sequestered by others.

A Poem of Unrest

Men duly understand the river of life,
misconstruing it, as it widens and its cities grow
dark and denser, always farther away.

And of course that remote denseness suits
us, as lambs and clover might have
if things had been built to order differently.

But since I don't understand myself, only segments
of myself that misunderstand each other, there's no
reason for you to want to, no way you could

even if we both wanted it. Do those towers even exist?
We must look at it that way, along those lines
so the thought can erect itself, like plywood battlements.

A Waking Dream

And the failing panopticon? That happened before,
when my uncle was in his bathrobe, on vacation.
Leastways, folks *said* it was a vacation . . .

Are you referring to your Uncle Obadiah,
the one that spent twenty years in the drunk-tank
and could whistle all the latest hits when sprung?
No one ever cared to talk much about it, it seemed a little *too*
peculiar, and he, he had forgotten the art
of knowing how far to go too far.

Just so. When driven, he would materialize in a Palm Beach suit
and Panama hat with tiny rainbow holes in it.
That was someone who knew how to keep up appearances
until he had exhausted them. Some of the railroad crew
got to know him at times, and could never figure out how he knew
exactly when a storm would hit. And when its anthracitic orgasm
erupted, we were out in the salley gardens mending coils
from the last big one. Such is my recollection. And vipers
would pause to notice. Meanwhile he was acting more and more

like a candidate. Then the wave of beach chairs crashed over us
and there was nothing more to be said for it. The case was closed,
it was "history," he liked to say, as though that were a topic
he could expand on if he chose, but it was more likely
to be night, and no one could extricate it properly.

Yet I had been told of an estimate.
That's what we don't know! If only I could get my senses
back in the right order, and had time to ponder this old message,

I could have the sluice-gates opened in a jiffy. As it is,
they're probably more than a little rusty, and do we know,
really know, as chasm-dwellers are said
to know, which way is upstream?

Abe's Collision

So much energy deployed
in circumnavigating the seer's collisions!
Don't do it yet,
it hasn't happened.
There is something in it.

And if we were a guidepost,
life would come along one day,

verify its balance, then leave
straight into the flustered ballooning of branches,
hands on the long ramp
leading to the restaurant with its coffee.

Sure, it's time we merged.
There are no others to do it
for us, we think we're nice.
That's why we've got to do it.
It takes balls to do it
and a heavy-duty sucker across the way.

A snake will unplug the drain.
The slate will light up and read itself.

Allotted Spree

How the past filled its designated space
with every kind of drollery, so there
were not just the things one knew about.

It's the secret of my gospel, it can never
be gone for too long or get too fancy.
Everybody wants to own a share in it!
This, too, is impossible.

I saw a woman in red move, come out from behind the brush.
I saw ten milky-white puppy dogs who chanted at me:
"You're a handful." I saw the spire of St. Diana's
prick and light up the sky. Those were gnashed doldrums.

Down where the last coitus happened,
another, a new madman in a cloak and hat,
was rising with the moon. They don't let you off
for these little things. Try imagining it.

Yes but against the sofa of your captivating lens
your appetites are wizard, dear. Let's give them all
a chance. On to the starboard
list of the apartment, to the gemstone-crusted tankard.

Andante Misterioso

The perfume climbs into my tree.
It is given to red-haired sprites:
words that music expresses
almost amply.
          The symphony at the station
then, and all over people trying to hear it
and others trying to get away. A "trying"
situation, perhaps, yet no one is worse off than before.

Horses slog through dirt—hell,
it's normal for 'em.

And that summer cottage we rented once—remember
how the bugs came in through the screens, and
all was not as it was supposed to be?
Nowadays people have cars for things like that,
to carry them away, I mean,
I suppose.
          And wherever man sets his giant foot
petals spring up, and artificial torsos,
dressmakers' dummies. And an ancient photograph
and an ancient phonograph, that carols

in mist. Pardon. The landlord locked us out.

Angels (you

know who you are), come back
when you've aged a little, when the outdoors
is an attractive curiosity no longer.
Don't get me wrong, I *like* your waving
turquoise mittens extantly. I must polish
my speech, having spent a life
watching old Steffi Duna movies, and being warned
about the consequences. It seems I should pass;
there's only one essay question, and it can be about anything
you like. Yet I hesitate, like a spermatozoid
that's lost its way and doesn't dare ask directions—
they'd club it if it did. Once you're en route
it doesn't matter if you know, besides, anyway.

Conversely the winter circuit closes down
until some time in spring, but more likely forever.
Signs of rot and corruption are everywhere
and are even copied by the fashion-conscious.
I must sugar my hair. And my factotum?

You said there was one more in your party.
No one is in a hurry.
Suddenly the day is crocus-sweet.

Anxiety and Hardwood Floors

Only a breath of this region
spindles me off and growing, yes, again.
How fine to be late in the season
where the hopeless hide their fetters
in chains of golden hair. Its air

wants nothing to do with any of us. Yet if I am
the strong man at the post office, as the clock's nine
o'clock tells me I am, why it will go better for the all
of us in here. This living
room he taunts me with. But everybody can see the
sun, abashed and unashamed, pummeling through the rusted
curtains. Pass me that box of gin,
will you?

At First I Thought I Wouldn't

Say Anything About It

but then I thought keeping quiet about it might appear even ruder.
At first I thought I had died and gone to heaven
but that scapegrace the unruly sun informed me otherwise.

I am in my heavyset pants and find this occupation of beekeeper charming
though I have yet to meet my first bee.
We don't know if I get to keep the hat and veil.

"Too hot," he said. "Too hot for everything!"
He so caring, so mundane. ". . . to have you on board."
Bulgarian choirs everywhere stood up and sang the song of the rent.
It was lovely. Now I shall take a short vacation,
proof that I am needed here. Nobody wants my two cents

anymore, I believe. To some it was like skating in summer.
A small turret perched over the lake. It exploded.
That's the way I feel about people taking me out
to some nice repast, and afterwards you go home and
go over everything that was stated. I prefer flowers and breathing.

At Liberty and Cranberry

The car bounds forward eagerly, and for a moment
it's like Madrid: a taste of cinnamon and something
almost too unimportant to mention. A sense of morning
without any of the particulars that morning is,
that it inhabits, all of them, individually.
And yes we invited the fish
over again to tell about high school and yes
he came apologetically and mentioned sodomy parenthetically
until we all played cards and it was time to go.

Everybody realized
there had been such a beautiful evening.

Yet if I want to take you on my lap
and be romantic—well, or use the word "romantic"
several times and bring up the faded question
of sentiment and sentimentality, like faded lips
on a post, I'm allowed to be only monastic and neat,

while the cute are always with us,
are all around us, out on the bay, the river,
like a miniature armada
with an ad on every sail.
Go back through here, it says,
you didn't come up this way, but through here
you'll find it's very nice.

And, unruffled, we do.

Atonal Music

The hamlet stroked its reflection in a
plum—it wasn't crooning now, not for generic
supplies, anyway. They are lowering hoops
from houses, the whole thing's very much up in the air.
I twiddle my thumbs in a doorway, look
out from time to time. It's fine to reminisce,
but no one really cares about your childhood,
not even you. It's not even that, or a past,
but an aesthetic remoteness blossoming profusely
but vaguely around what *does*
stand out here and there: a window square, a bone
left by an intrepid dog. You own
them but may not appreciate them—they're
too mortal for that, for you.

I woke in the night to hear a runnel
coursing down my mansard—damn!
I'd left the trapdoor ratcheted. It all
smears me, like scenery. I can
only be ambient.

They observed me once, you know.

Awful Effects of Two Comets

There will not always be a step
to the undoing of the rightness you now so justly feel

in the edge of Hong Kong where it's all right to buy spirits. The
canal crowd threw fetters at him.
Then there will not always be a stair
to punish the unborn and the boy who said he'd rather

do it on another day. There is a chair,
its arms rubbed almost bare from excess living.
There is a fan I think over there.

Otherwise we make no money off them.
They're not worth importing, only to smoke
the tips of and then the whole magazine
goes up, to some surprise and cheers
on the part of petite nudist pedestrians

who can make nothing rise,
not even your eyes, which, seriously, I love
staring at and making love to:
I, a merchant from over the hill
with hunger and a big cow to fill.

. . . *by an Earthquake*

A hears by chance a familiar name, and the name involves a riddle of the past.

B, in love with A, receives an unsigned letter in which the writer states that she is the mistress of A and begs B not to take him away from her.

B, compelled by circumstances to be a companion of A in an isolated place, alters her rosy views of love and marriage when she discovers, through A, the selfishness of men.

A, an intruder in a strange house, is discovered; he flees through the nearest door into a windowless closet and is trapped by a spring lock.

A is so content with what he has that any impulse toward enterprise is throttled.

A solves an important mystery when falling plaster reveals the place where some old love letters are concealed.

A-4, missing food from his larder, half believes it was taken by a "ghost."

A, a crook, seeks unlawful gain by selling A-8 an object, X, which A-8 already owns.

A sees a stranger, A-5, stealthily remove papers, X, from the pocket of another stranger, A-8, who is asleep. A follows A-5.

A sends an infernal machine, X, to his enemy, A-3, and it falls into the hands of A's friend, A-2.

Angela tells Philip of her husband's enlarged prostate, and asks for money.

Philip, ignorant of her request, has the money placed in an escrow account.

A discovers that his pal, W, is a girl masquerading as a boy.

A, discovering that W is a girl masquerading as a boy, keeps the knowledge to himself and does his utmost to save the masquerader from annoying experiences.

A, giving ten years of his life to a miserly uncle, U, in exchange for a
college education, loses his ambition and enterprise.

A, undergoing a strange experience among a people weirdly deluded,
discovers the secret of the delusion from Herschel, one of the
victims who has died. By means of information obtained from
the notebook, A succeeds in rescuing the other victims of the
delusion.
A dies of psychic shock.
Albert has a dream, or an unusual experience, psychic or otherwise,
which enables him to conquer a serious character weakness and
become successful in his new narrative, "Boris Karloff."

Silver coins from the Mojave Desert turn up in the possession of a
sinister jeweler.
Three musicians wager that one will win the affections of the local
kapellmeister's wife; the losers must drown themselves in a nearby
stream.
Ardis, caught in a trap and held powerless under a huge burning glass,
is saved by an eclipse of the sun.
Kent has a dream so vivid that it seems a part of his waking experience.
A and A-2 meet with a tragic adventure, and A-2 is killed.
Elvira, seeking to unravel the mystery of a strange house in the hills,
is caught in an electrical storm. During the storm the house van-
ishes and the site on which it stood becomes a lake.
Alphonse has a wound, a terrible psychic wound, an invisible psychic
wound, which causes pain in flesh and tissue which, otherwise,
are perfectly healthy and normal.
A has a dream which he conceives to be an actual experience.
Jenny, homeward bound, drives and drives, and is still driving, no
nearer to her home than she was when she first started.

Petronius B. Furlong's friend, Morgan Windhover, receives a wound from which he dies.

Thirteen guests, unknown to one another, gather in a spooky house to hear Toe reading Buster's will.

Buster has left everything to Lydia, a beautiful Siamese girl poet of whom no one has heard.

Lassie and Rex tussle together politely; Lassie, wounded, is forced to limp home.

In the Mexican gold rush a city planner is found imprisoned by outlaws in a crude cage of sticks.

More people flow over the dam and more is learned about the missing electric cactus.

Too many passengers have piled onto a cable car in San Francisco; the conductor is obliged to push some of them off.

Maddalena, because of certain revelations she has received, firmly resolves that she will not carry out an enterprise that had formerly been dear to her heart.

Fog enters into the shaft of a coal mine in Wales.

A violent wind blows the fog around.

Two miners, Shawn and Hillary, are pursued by fumes.

Perhaps Emily's datebook holds the clue to the mystery of the seven swans under the upas tree.

Jarvis seeks to manage Emily's dress shop and place it on a paying basis. Jarvis's bibulous friend, Emily, influences Jarvis to take to drink, scoffing at the doctor who has forbidden Jarvis to indulge in spirituous liquors.

Jarvis, because of a disturbing experience, is compelled to turn against his friend, Emily.

A ham has his double, "Donnie," take his place in an important enterprise.

Jarvis loses his small fortune in trying to help a friend.

Lodovico's friend, Ambrosius, goes insane from eating the berries of a strange plant, and makes a murderous attack on Lodovico.

"New narrative" is judged seditious. Hogs from all over go squealing down the street.

Ambrosius, suffering misfortune, seeks happiness in the companionship of Joe, and in playing golf.

Arthur, in a city street, has a glimpse of Cathy, a strange woman who has caused him to become involved in a puzzling mystery.

Cathy, walking in the street, sees Arthur, a stranger, weeping.

Cathy abandons Arthur after he loses his money and is injured and sent to a hospital.

Arthur, married to Beatrice, is haunted by memories of a former sweetheart, Cornelia, a heartless coquette whom Alvin loves.

Sauntering in a park on a fine day in spring, Tricia and Plotinus encounter a little girl grabbing a rabbit by its ears. As they remonstrate with her, the girl is transformed into a mature woman who regrets her feverish act.

Running up to the girl, Alvin stumbles and loses his coins.

In a nearby dell, two murderers are plotting to execute a third.

Beatrice loved Alvin before he married.

B, second wife of A, discovers that B-3, A's first wife, was unfaithful.

B, wife of A, dons the mask and costume of B-3, A's paramour, and meets A as B-3; his memory returns and he forgets B-3, and goes back to B.

A discovers the "Hortensius," a lost dialogue of Cicero, and returns it to the crevice where it lay.

Ambrose marries Phyllis, a nice girl from another town.

Donnie and Charlene are among the guests invited to the window.
No one remembers old Everett, who is left to shrivel in a tower.
Pellegrino, a rough frontiersman in a rough frontier camp, undertakes
    to care for an orphan.
Ildebrando constructs a concealed trap, and a person near to him,
    Gwen, falls into the trap and cannot escape.

By Guess and by Gosh

Even so, we have forgotten their graves.
I swear to you I will not beat one drum in your absence.

And the beasts of night will not forget their crimes,
nor the others their roly-polyness.

It was in a garage where tire irons jangled in the breeze
to the accompaniment of flyswatters functioning
that we first heard of that Phoenician sailor
and how when the tide was out he would pretend to be
the Flying Dutchman on one of his infrequent shore leaves
to garner a spouse. But he was all red with jewels—
not rubies, cheap gems. And his incisors struck fear
in the hearts of the entourage. Nevertheless, many
were the maidens who considered him an option,
though they always ended by rejecting it. Some said it was his breath,
others, the driven cornsilk of his hair. Perhaps
it was the lack of something called "personable,"
though I think I don't even want to know what that is, I'll follow
my heart over warm oceans of Chinese lounge music
until the day the badger coughs up that secret,
though first we must discover the emetic,
the one I told you about.

Confused minions swarmed on the quarterdeck.
No one was giving orders anymore. In fact it was quite a while
since any had been issued. Who's in charge here?
Can't anyone stop the player piano before it rolls us
in the trough of a tidal wave? How did we get to be so many?
I wonder what's playing at the local movie theater.

Some Hitchcock or other, for there are many fanciers
in these unsightly parts. And who would want mothers
for supper?

Can You Hear, Bird

And for all the days it doesn't happen
something does happen,
solid and nutritional like a wrapped steak
tossed on a counter. At first I couldn't believe the thirst;

soon, so soon, it becomes average and airy,
a fixture. Precept to be toyed with.
The road started to get rough with me.
A mere 800 feet away the car wept
on its blocks
and little Peter came and looked around and went away.

It was kind of a mistake and he went away.

It was a kind mistake, breezes over dashboard.
Twin violins sew
a fine seam;
a paw slips over the face of the clock,
laggards and dudgeons in between.

All I meant to suggest was the negative of what has
been done surges and slops against fifth-floor windows
in the time it takes to anchor a tricycle.
And we full of such courtesy,
blind to the days and it seems their systems the night,
teetering on a board's edge;
sure and the unrolled film fans out
in suns like a dolphin or a skate's wing.
After all who blubbered the truth
It wasn't I

Cantilever

I knew we should have stopped back there
by the pudding station
but the pudding people were so—well—
full of themselves.

The Sphinx didn't want us to come this far
even though we answered her questions
and threw in a bonus answer: "As honey is to the jaguar."

And we so well all along too—

Coming up is the world's longest single cantilever span.
I am numb with thrips.

Chapter II, Book 35

He was a soldier or a Shaker. At least he was doing *something*,
going somewhere. Often, in the evenings, he'd rant about Mark Twain,
how that wasn't his real name, and was he hiding something?
If so, then why call himself a humorist?
We began to tire of his ravings, but (as so often happens)
it was just at that point that a salient character trait
revealed itself, or rather, manifested itself within him.
It was one of those goofy days in August
when all men (and some women) dream of chocolate sodas.
He confessed he'd had one for lunch,
then took us out to the street to show us the whir and dazzle
of living in some other city, where so much that is different goes on.
I guess he was inspired by Lahore. Said it came to him
in his dreams every night. And little by little
we felt ourselves being transported there. Not that we wanted
to be there, far from that. But we were either too timid
or unaware to urge him otherwise. Then he mentioned Timbuktu.
Said he'd actually been there, that the sidewalks were pink
and the huts made of mother-of-pearl, not mud, as is commonly
supposed. Said he'd had the best venison and apple tart
in his life there.
                    Well, we were accompanying him in the daze
that usually surrounded him, when we began to think about ourselves:
When *was* the last time we had done so? And the stranger shifted
        shape
again (he was now wearing a Zouave's culottes), and asked us
would we want to *live* in Djibouti, or Providence, or Lyon, now that
we'd seen them, and we chorused (like frogs), Oh no, we
want to live in New York, not that the other places aren't as splendid
and interesting as you say. It's just that New York

feels more like home to us. It's ugly, it's dirty, the people are rude
(kind and rude), and every surface has a fine film of filth
on it that behooves slobs like us, and will in time turn to diamonds,
just like the mother-of-pearl shacks in Timbuktu. And he said,
You know I was wrong about Mark Twain. It was his real name,
and he was a humorist, a genuine American humorist for the ages.

Chronic Symbiosis

These things can be arranged, he said.
Besides, glitter has become reasonable again.
Hadn't you heard? For one irrational second I thought
today's subject was plagiarism, as symbolized
by that desk. But no, it's joy
in never knowing, in having once known,
and in its still not being too late to know.
Yes, but I know now that I knew
long ago when children
around me grew. Some I liked, others
probably not as much. And from that the road to living sped
ever onward, brambles in its hair, dark patches
under the trees where no moon was. Which means I guess
I can summon all objects from their shelves,
sucked with us into the vacuum-cleaner bag
the open road is. Quick, tell me a story

that I may repeat it with minor variations
and the job be over. Rakes and shovels lean beside
the open door this evening with a special luster
all their own, that they can't know. And I,

I was spirited away by a handsome enchanter
to a medium-sized city not twenty miles from here
and live my life as I can hear and smell it. No grouch
am I, yet hardly an earth-mother either. That's
what befalls most of us plagiarists. We write steadily
away in a barn, with straw and barn swallows for company,
mindless of inspiration or imagination. We have everything
we need for today. We can feed it to crows.

Collected Places

When you come on,
     I respond more sweetly.
But the key is laced in
     a travesty,
much like the dead man's cane.

For generations I went to bed because I was asleep.
Something overt about the silence
and how we traded its futures
for chameleons, shenanigans.
I feel as though I just woke up,

which of course I just did,
my head at your thigh.
Is there any place known to the coast,
I mean *this* one, that rides
us so severely, yanking the bridle,
digging its stirrups in, that will leave
a pine forest and jam in the holes in the sieve
of my memory, when the adders have slept?
Order it then open,
longitude stricken from the record.

And where is the dismal mouse
that will affront me for so little?
There is retching in the sky,
a blue pencil box
for the sores we own and still wear,
a nodding as of rabbits, or storks.

And the head is still miles away.

I fear you cannot read this.
I shall make amends
in some other book, but not today,
not until the horseless carriage is reinvented
in the free land of our screams
and the remainder can be calculated
exactly, morning and confrontational cliffs,
a place you want to hear.

Coming Down from New York

The harshness isn't intentional.
It's the dark side of these frightful enterprises
that would otherwise leave us washed by the sun
in extravagant attitudes, situations
only the insufficiently trained ought to try.

Dangerous Moonlight

Of course you will. It happens even after you're dead.
Or, in some cases, the results are positive, but the verdict
negative. "In such a muddle," you said, and "all muddled up."
I wish I could help but I've a million things to do
and restoring your peace of mind isn't one of them. There goes my
    phone . . .

The professor's opinion on all this was: "Well, he leaps around,
doesn't he, your little surgeon-poet. Seems to lead an agitated life
on the surface, but if you really listen to him you find he's got
everything down pat. Knows where his bread is buttered, and his ass.
I could open a drawer of rhetorical footnotes, translated from
the Japanese or Old Church Slavonic, if I felt like it, and in there'd
be something that rhymes with him and his coziness, his following the
    trail
all the way back to its point of origin. Plus his lively friendliness, which
coexists, numinously I grant, with a desire to inflict harm.

There is a poetry in mere existence,
the kind that shopkeepers and people walking along the street lead,
you know, and evenness, that fills them up to whatever brim
is there, and stays, transient, all the days of their lives.
Such enharmonics are not for your poet-person. He sees, and breeds:
Otherwise the game isn't worth the candle to him. He'd as soon rhyme
    breeze
with breathes, as walk over to that fire hydrant in the grass
to examine it, see what it's made of, make sure it's not an idea in some
philosopher's mind, that will bruise and cloud over once that mind's
removed, leaving but a dubious trace of itself, like a ring of puffball
    dust . . ."

Suppose we grant its power of conserving to listening,
so it's really a full-fledged element in the creative process.
Well, others have done just that from time immemorial,
when women wore tall cones on their heads with sails attached to
    them.
But, as mattering ages, it hardens into something smooth like good
    luck,
no longer kinetic. Then you can listen all you want
at palace doors, creaky vents . . .

This imploring process is twofold. First, let's not forget its root
in implosive. That's something it's got up its sleeve.
Did you ever see an anarchist without his round bomb?
And then the someone that's got to be implored,
how does he fit in? I'll tell you: like a wedge that was subtracted
from a wheel of cheese, and is replaced, so that it fits perfectly;
no one can see where the cut was. Well, that's
poetic argument for you. It stands on its own ("The cheese stands
    alone"),
but can at the drop of a speculation be seen again as a part,
a vital one, of the mucus cloud that is generalized human thought
    aimed at
a quarrel or a rebus in the lining. And that's the way
we get old with poetry. Comes a time when no one has a notion
of anything else, and the odor of fried brains contends
with the damp of vacant ancestral halls, to their mutual
betterment, actually. Here, hand me that cod . . .

Debit Night

We were coming down from the city the city is where you come when you don't want to listen or be excused from listening. It is a hard hat out and some days "stiletto" heels—but who told you about hat we don't know about hat too much or about how "hat" grows. Coming down we passed through a former violet producing center. Around World War I there were maybe a hundred violet farms in this region of New York state conducive to violets. It is a very labor intensive thing now there are no longer any except one or two. Up until the end of World War II it was the fashion for ladies to wear bunches of violets but then

it changed. Now no one had any use for them. Now everyone likes violets I don't see. Yes but you don't see anybody wearing them or buying any. Some even think of them as weeds. Nevertheless the former violet business has left its trace in place-names here such as Violet Lane and Violet Hill. They are beautiful aren't they until you stop to think that violets could be weeds and of a reason why nobody buys them anymore. Yes but I will still think the

names

A sandbox sometimes had weeds growing in it including one that looked like a dandelion only it was tall and thrifty. Always was the sand more beautiful after the rain when there was a dried wet crust on top with pebblelike pores starring its surface. But mostly it was out of sight. There was not a window of the house where it wasn't around the corner so naturally it is seen less and thus gets worn into the mind like a crease in a road map that has been folded up the wrong way too many times.

Jana prefers the city. Says there's more light in it, or the light gets divided up by the streets more so a little goes a long way. Light is something that should not be wasted so as to produce its maximum effect as it is even on some boulevards where it stretches out too much, too wide and too long into the future. This is true but in the country it gets more soaked up in the bushes and buildings so a little more is always required and a little more is all there is. In the city you can eavesdrop on brick walls and this is called "repointing." What comes up in the inevitable ensuing conversation is sure funny but doesn't look ahead to the future of philosophy or decide how life should ultimately be lived. There is no conversation even about half-serious things like the theater. Instead everybody makes a unique little mess like a child shitting in its pants that's proud of it. The auto horns scare everything near away anyhow. The place pivots; this has already been patented. You can go down to sleep by the river or in a movie. See that boat? It's real.

So after we had done the chores and brought back living to the house there was something on its mind like a ball of yarn. Yes, a ball of yarn is what is there as I wanted to say. Say, stay anyway will you? I might. I've got things to do. Yes, but this is one of them. That's true. But I still have things to do I might go. Oh no you're not. Oh no? Okay then I really will stay because I want to really. Really she said? Then I will show you this dried crust of bread which is the truth, you must never forget it. Oh I never will I said it's what I wanted all along. How many acres do you want? Oh I never sought them they always came to me until quite recently. Indeed? Well here comes another one it's green or black. It must be yours she said. You played the mandrake right. Yes well here comes another and a whole lot of them. By George she said we should have been ready for them, but that's the way it is you can't be and you are. Think of World War I, it's green and black and surely there was less daylight around then, more fog and boats on the East River with people lining up to go on them. Yes it was a premonition of these our times she said and so I conjure you, don't go around telling what you know to people, you are likely to get it back. Then peace, of a sort? The high-minded sun combs the tallest man-made structures on earth and then you get a little peace and some darkness down in the lobbies where everything begins to happen. No one in his handsome and enduring stable. Just having to endure is like going for the jugular but it should be a caravanserai. The problem is to get over what is being endured but hasn't been and to make for the middle distance, after the teacups and primulas but before philosophy and "last things," where thighs shine astride dim neighboring curbs and strangers greet you convulsively. These are more last things, I think, to think about

all along along what I wanted all along

Do Husbands Matter?

Let's get this going again. It might work. To ask pardon . . .

These days I am much on the cliffs. I like cliffs. They lead to

a nice breeze . . .

Forests of fire hatch the soupstone factory.
When they get infected they tend to gyrate,
sometimes a lot.

Trees come to stand in for the scenery that's missing.
Well, and what might that be? Well, trees of course. The occasional
    shrub.
The windjammer's jammed again. Solemn, small porticoes.
Stone steps leading down into the ground. Potatoes.
And you don't even know them.

Did it seem perfect then?

The townside, sea of troubles, value, money.
Dr. Driscoll will be here soon
with his decoder. Meanwhile, everybody
just stand still. If yawl
don't move it will summon the laser legs.
In a matter of hours we can be on the high seas
where marriages are consummated
and amazon drummers croon
and we encounter the order of the day.

At last, we can split hairs.

I needn't remind you how much of the mirror-ball is in this, nor
how such states are very much the exception to the general rule of not
    interfering.
Even then the interpersonal
has been around, hedges its bets
as though this were a matter of some gravity,
though no one can stake it out, or even know
very well what it happens to be.
This much I could hesitantly aver
and turn into a saga, that melts next day
like an iceberg towed into tropical waters.
That's an unusual boat: wearied-seeming,
caught in the cleft of a dream,
or is it something you just wear, like diaries
on special occasions, while welcomes are wearing out
and tall men have come to eat
mattress-insides, this time.

O the woman lay in the longboat.

Sometimes it comes from even farther back.

Dull Mauve

Twenty miles away, in the colder
waters of the Atlantic, you gaze longingly
toward the coast. Didn't you once love someone
there? Yes, but it was only a cat, and I,
a manatee, what could I do? There are no rewards
in this world for pissing your life away, even
if it means you get to see forgotten icebergs
of decades ago peeling off from the mass
to dive under the surface, raising a
mountain of seething glass before they lunge back up
to start the unknown perilous journey
to the desolate horizon.

       That was the way
I thought of each day when I was young, a sloughing-off,
both suicidal and imbued with a certain ritual grace.
Later, there were so many protagonists
one got quite lost, as in a forest of doppelgängers.
Many things were going on. And the moon, poised
on the ridge like an enormous, smooth grapefruit, understood
the importance of each and wasn't going
to make one's task any easier, though we loved her.

Eternity Sings the Blues

Music lovers everywhere
endorse it—just thought I'd let
you know it's National Frivolity Week
again. Will they ever get done
with these things? Stop commercializing 'em?

Music and worry—the two most terrible
things a man can know. How about
women? Strangely, they come off better
just by observing things. This hundred-year-old
inkstone is evidence enough of that. How so?

But music, played by a gifted child,
is just about the finest thing anywhere.
Puts me in mind of a cigar
I smoked in a picket line once. They all thought
the boss hired me to do it. Now I ask you.
But I kept on smoking. The point is, when you spot
worry, you have to move straight in through
the flanks it invariably leaves unprotected.
I am cussed now,
more worse than ever, yet I never
bequeathed an orange to an orphan,
or padlocks to a mechanic. I had too much
to do, too much fun getting out of there
into another house of which I remember little.
Oh the places I've lived. Airplanes to London,
and then it was hard not to uproot the rancid
stalk of romanticism, so I left it there
as an experiment. Soon the fairies was buzzing
round my head. I got out of there *real* fast.

Why do these dreams of worry plague you?
You seem like such a comfortable man.
Aye, I am that, but I'm also terrible
in the northeast. Wasn't it D. W. Griffith
who said, "You don't know what it's like to have a big nose"?
And so we dream some of the same dreams,
him and me together—of kitchens, and bushes outside 'em,
and a woman who hides behind a tree,
waiting for the keyboard of her youth to unravel
in unsightly seams over the pavement.
Absolutely nothing he or she does
escapes my vigilant attention. But if you'll wait here
I'll go over and see what that car wants.
Oh stop that—now you really are
learning to be boring. Soon no one will want you
except for the occasional syphilitic barmaid,
and then what will your urine tests prove?
Better a spotted record than a tarnished silver thread
I always tells them. It's true, nobody will unveil me.
I've slept with my feet in the spittoon, with only
a pair of chopsticks for a pillow.
I've been deferred. And all because some runt
of a chameleon put a curse on me once, mixing me
up with his oafish brother-in-law.
Is that any way to begin a life?
And long after my Enoch Arden–like return
to the world of discos and lemon groves, his words
return to haunt me still: Avast,
ye pantyhose-wearing, portmanteau-carrying,
bleached-out denizen! Return to the sea that vomited you
on its shore one fatal August afternoon. Begone!

So must I carry this paddle
forever, until I find a sucker who'll buy it
for less than I paid for it. So runs this carousel
we call life.

Yet for those not snookered
by it, a fatal balm mollifies
susceptibility to drafts, and mild
allergies, or are they transgressions in disguise?
Better to sleep on the docks
than in the linen closet of privilege, always
wondering what it was that woke you—I've known
that routine too, like a serial killer
with nothing on his mind, who couldn't make eye contact
with you for all the gold in Scotland Yard.
You think of yourselves as having lived
a life of amused tolerance, woozy
with doubts, at times, but buoyed by your
delusion that all this, guarded moments and all,
is part of some life-affirming élan vital. Well,
I'm here to tell you you're as doomed as the hoariest
chink or octoroon, or the "anthropophagi,
and men whose heads do grow beneath their shoulders."
Would anyone like this oar? The special ends tomorrow.

Often over the bluff-infested coasts a warm
zephyr breathes. We forget about memorizing
our parts and retreat to the dressing room,
silly with relief and grief. What! Was it for this
I squeezed the tubes of paint
on your pristine palette, and is it

that I am going to be rewarded by something
other than a fatal sting? And the lads
and lassies assure you that such is the case, that
in any event no one ever escapes the swimming pool
without being shriveled to a prunelike consistency.
O beaters, how did you find my forest?
What will you do if I stay here
just for the hell of it? In any case
it's getting late, cat burglars are astir, and something
smokelike in the wind. I'll be
off now, the tide is running, the ship
writhing in the roads, and I must finish
my diary by midnight, or be fated
to continue this life into the next. O
brothers, sisters, friends, catamites—
it's been a long and intelligent journey, hasn't it?
If I ever found myself here again I'd do something
about fixing the holes in the landscape
and healing the sick, though there's about
as much chance of that as finding a used lottery ticket in a dungheap.
Tell you what—
you continue on the road to House Beautiful
and I'll strain my eyes in their sockets looking
for a single white wave of a hand in the distance
as my train speeds by. I was told not to get
into any of this, not to talk about where I
came from, or my mission here, but I'm tempted
to share a few secrets with you, though I guess I won't.

Remember me to those assholes the judge
and the bailiff. Speak kindly of me to gossip columnists,

praising the achievements I was once noted for, that are
sprouting like Roquefort, or a zinc tree. OK,
worry, I'll catch up to you in a minute, once I've
dusted off my shoes and finished adulating myself,
adoring my stretched reflection in the funhouse mirror,
and stopped handing out tracts that look like Chinese
takeout menus. I'm both bogus
and bold. Not to put too fine a point on it.

Fascicle

No one ever had to face such turmoil
in these days of riots and student demonstrations.
Don't bet on it. "No one the governor recruits
ever passes muster," she said. "And painted rooms are bonny."

Nevertheless, I opened my attaché case.
"It's enough to fluster
Hercule Poirot or Inspector Javert. Why,
it almost seems as if we are arriving

in a port of Cyprus, the damaged
storm in ruins, past the mole
and the breakwater to the incredible piles
of volcanic tuff no one esteems, if indeed

we're here. Let's see, my flotation mask
is in order, ditto my Cypriot currency (dinars,
no doubt—isn't everybody?). My cocktail and ticket
are perfect. Not so the drops of sweat beading my

headband, but no one cares what you look like—
it's appearances that count. But here in this
cultural demimonde I've been banished to, they'll seize on anything:
earrings, a trace of luster on the broad swath

of evening, signed by a renowned couturier. If it weren't
for living, that is being alongside almost everything
that happens and hearing thirdhand about the rest, we'd all
have rotted at our moorings eons ago, sunk to the mucky

bottom of this cretinous ocean. Say, did he tell you the one
about the flea and the cabdriver picking his nose,
or has he saved you for more august reunions,
under a turtle moon, its starched sheaves heaving? In truth

he knew not to what saint to address himself
when the last panhandler buzzed into view.
That were a churring time." Beats me, I mean
why we're not to make more of it, if you

know what I mean . . .

Five O'Clock Shadow

I

Don't just stand there, Kiki.
You're onstage. They're all looking at you.

"Along life's weary path I glide . . ."

Leda, when it came time
to consider the swan's suggestion, humbled
her braces, brought success to heel.

Tell her half the story.

Then weeping on these shoals,
like an enchantress extruded
in bar light, overturned the fashion
shoot, brought dumb heterodoxy
out into the open:

"For seven years I twisted the splint
till the pain grew more or less correct.
I should die in the right page."

II

Another time we were digging a fire trench.
Along came a fireball,
stopped, asked the time of day
and went politely on his way.

In the house they looked out:
Yet another hour had come;
the alcoves were deep with remembrance,
remembered piety. A woman offered fruit
mechanically. It's just like the games of my day
which no one can authenticate anymore:
How many times do you kick the can?
How long must you remain blindfolded?
And we knew the flag was a friend,
forgotten ceremony, nailed to the floor,
climbing, tooth by tooth.

From the Observatory

When they had climbed the Valley of Thieves
and rested at the aleatory base camp
a horseshoe moon began to pierce the curtain of dreams.

It seemed there was something wrong with everything.
The greenhouse was ethereal and too far away.
A gnat ignited the harbor; it rose up gold and sloppy,
with too many seals to think about. The basement
was a dirigible. The Home Counties bristled at suggestions
of voyeurism and venery: "Was it for this you came?
To watch us writhe and cringe? Are you happy,
knowing the palace janissaries have subdued us?"

The cult of personality issued conflicting commands
that managed to puddle every surface.
It's like it was before the flood: Nothing
is dry enough or wet enough. What's needed is a sense
of invitation, to this or some other domed picnic.
But since we're here, we might as well memorize the rules
for future reference. All other details
are as the exterior of this wall that reared us: ancient,
trapped in an understanding of the present, where submarines
gather, and eavesdroppers ply their trade.

                                    And the riddle
unknotted itself; the second agreeable ordeal began.

Fuckin' Sarcophagi

And when they had mounted it on the flatbed,
the dogfish requested a commuter's ticket. I'm no longer feeling
any of it. Generations of toppled heads
have come home to roost in my priory.
The smell of doughnuts frying offers them minimal
support.

All those years with the tree's rings growing around me,
the leaves in my face, branches obstructing others,
have learned me how one deaf animal forgets another
in the rush to light. And there on the threshold it forgets
its name, its very purpose. And allows septic deviance
to whittle away at the formatted intertext.
It's as well the hygrometer was swallowed
by a tusked creature, as we never came here at all.
All those suds on the porch and the front walk
only meant that baby likes to blow soap bubbles
when not involved in anything more strenuous,
such as teething. She sees through the holes in my coat
imaginable dapper Dans who one day will become part and parcel
of the AstroTurf.

When I wonder weather it's over between us, ever over,
why, a shy spiral announces your cue:
You too are to have nothing to do
for the next five hours.
Look, I've packed lunch . . .

Betimes the *bêtises* fall where they may.

Getting Back In

Melodies of the past, fibers, tangled tracings . . .
Getting back in is the easy part.
Being stuck in today isn't.

What is this "today" you speak of so incessantly?

It's where the rubber meets the road and they discuss
in one long fawning kiss. It's the posse's
new poster child. It's . . . My system was downloaded
but bogus retorts are still coming out of it.
It's pleasures and palaces. A commitment.

This is where the road tires and all vehicles
instinctively lean toward some breakdown lane
or other but there aren't any. The police,
of course, are aware of this but don't let on.

I see where someone was put in prison just for dreaming.
Sixteen long years. And when they let them out,
they go back to it. It's as natural for them as copper moths
or striped cabanas in the rain forest. You do have got to
give credit to the organizers, though. Without them this whole thing
would be as chaotic as a clambake. And us with no spirits,
no place left to land. No airport wants us.
And if we get juiced and relax everybody wants us
for purposes of synchronicity. A single item is too many,
but a pair is just fine, they say.

Well, I've had it with the 'burbs.
From where I sit I can see hundreds of freight cars,

some of them painted bright colors, but mostly
they are of a dark sort of color.
It's so lissom, the light! Rabbits everywhere . . .

Gladys Palmer

Do not go into Hawaii.
Even the price tags are afraid.
A bunch of wetsuits slapped a utility pole.
Something like a pupil
accosted me across from the mill.
The new wave of hijackings
resembles the others only in intensity. Otherwise, forget it.

We sanded the floors
and invited the ocean in.
The yellow pages promised free ginseng,
and a glorious spring morning
eloped with a tired, dirty afternoon from the end of winter.
Bubbles issued from people's mouths
before the solons could do anything about it.
It was foul to be afoot then, or a trick knee.

The man and the woman wondered:
Shit, what *about* the lost amulet?
What about it? Closer than the side
of this week's truncheon, communicable
as today's newspaper, yet everybody
got a piece to take home: The difference was significant.
I told the truth (it's best), but unfortunately I *was* the truth.
Come along, we'll forget till tomorrow
feet over these smooth pebbles, the prisoner's
last question.

Heavenly Arts Polka

She wasn't having one of her strange headaches tonight.
Whose fault is it? For a long time I thought it was mine,
blamed myself for every minor variation in the major upheaval.
Then . . .

It may have been the grass praying
for renewal, even though it meant their death,
the individual blades, and, as though psychic,
a white light hovered just above the lake's layer
like a photograph of ectoplasm.

Those are all fakes, aren't they?
In slow-moving traffic a man acts like he's going to be hit
by the stream of cars coming at him from both directions.
Like a cookie cutter, a streamroller lops the view off.

There are nine sisters, nine deafening knocks on the door,
nine busboys to be bussed—er, tipped. And in the thievery
of my own dreams I can see the square like a crystal,
the only imaginary thing we were meant to have,
now soiled, turned under
like a frayed shirt collar
a mother stitches for her son who's away at school,
mindful he may not care, may wear
another's scarlet-and-sulfur raiment
just so he take part in the academy fun.

And later, after the twister, slowly
we mixed drinks of the sort
that may be slopped only on script-girls, like lemonade.

Who knows what the world's got up its sleeve
next brunch, as long as you will be a part of me and all what I am
doing?

Hegel

Like a coffee table, the chair slides
across the polished floor—its aides have brushed its sides
again. How it shines! Hugs are interspersed with kisses;
the scrofulous interfaces with the electric clock.
It certainly is midnight
and for once it was early.

She said she had "dishpan hands"—no one
quite understood what she was talking about, yet issues
were skirted, no questions raised. Now when a peacock
stares out of the barnyard, no one mistakes it for a Christmas-tree
    ornament,
goes up to it and says, I liked you better in felt,
or was it at the Rangoon racetrack? But a bird
always has the last word.

I Saw No Need

I saw no need to paint the sky,
to cheer the runners passing by,
to let the lovely forest bleed.
I saw no need.

I saw no need to argue writs
with one who in a courtroom sits.
I saw the folly princes breed,
who saw no need.

I saw no need to cancel love—
Heavens, what was I thinking of?
I cannot read what others read.
I see no need.

I know the earth is out of whack.
I pine for boys whose name is Jack
who never pause to spill their seed.
They see no need.

And when visible day is done
all start to run. Stand up
to it. They stand up to you.
Hey, you never know.

I came upon a birch tree once,
a softly swaying silver dunce
in whose black branches mist had spread,
and gazed, and left it there for dead.

I saw no need t'explain myself
as others have concerning pelf.
This ditty bland seduces me.
Enough! I'll leave it by the tree,
the idling birch.

I saw no need to go to church
yet wearily I there did lurch
from time to time, and in the end
I felt its body like a friend.

Soon I forgot my mission's itch
and at the same time ceased to bitch.
Ineffable beauty where are you
I said I'm coming for you

and even if we don't match up
eventually we'll catch up
one to the other, comparing notes
or jotting down our favorite quotes.

All passion's spent; the evening dew
comes transitorily into view.
Tomorrow it will evaporate
and morning tigers seal its fate.

So, when it comes to choosing sides,
You be the one who's using guides.
Refreshed, I'll to my perch return
and leave these cherries in the urn.

I, Too

Happy thoughts weren't made to last,
but it is their compactness that eludes us.

The built-in obsolescence of every nanny, every pram,
is a force from God that issues from us.

How could we not like it, watching it emanate
like a breath of witch hazel
or a grayish-purple shroud?

Something has got to be done to the way we feel
before we get completely numb, like a colossus
floundering in its own wake.

See these hands?
Really we must make it up to them
or they'll take credit for everything we've accomplished
which they will anyway.

And what's-his-face can sit on his porch burping
uninterruptedly—propriety isn't hardy in this zone,
but that's not his problem. In fact
he doesn't have a problem. We, who see
around corners, into strongboxes, must wear
the guilt of our glancing. It's another appurtenance,
like a birdhouse or dishwasher, that we came to terms with
eons ago, when a tsunami of slime collided
with our pink stucco skyscraper. We know so much we've
kept it all in. That may be changing.

In an Inchoate Place

I

Is there another person you would like me to invite?
I shall, you know,
if only for the exquisite confusion it causes in you,
like a rope of starfish, tonight.

Opinion is divided on the merits of the majority of the guests.
The siblings are standardized but substandard:
red tadpoles lisping.

II

They are all free to come and go as they please
through the vanilla-flavored venetian blinds.

In Old Oklahoma

A tad triste I too found it,
along with other November matters that need not
concern us here. But what's wrong with here? Suffice it
to say baroque street gangs were breaking up

thanks to the same principles that oversaw their gestation.
A meaningless scuffle or shuffle ensued.
One wondered which stamps were licked, what tea poured
from on high as negative celebration

of all that is lost to us now, and all that is to come—
mysterious hybrids, most likely, veined purple pods
growing out of control to no one's detriment—I insist
on that. And then it rained fat rabbits—I

should have listened to my dog. In all,
another pleasant institution, like so many
pavilions that asterisk the harbor rim.
In all my life it was my twentieth birthday,

she came over; the night is all stuttering
orange flares and fig-colored queries
in the margin—it starts like this. It's breathless
and out of hope, a quartet for someone

semantics will never graze, nor the idling,
puny zephyrs, the last saviors one thinks of
looking to. Old Mother Hubbard knew nothing of pain
that flows as fondly as conversation among acquaintances,

and as discreetly.

Like a Sentence

How little we know,
and when we know it!

It was prettily said that "No man
hath an abundance of cows on the plain, nor shards
in his cupboard." Wait! I think I know who said that! It was . . .

Never mind dears, the afternoon
will fold you up, along with preoccupations
that now seem so important, until only a child
running around on a unicycle occupies center stage.
Then what will you make of walls? And I fear you
will have to come up with something,

be it a terraced gambit above the sea
or gossip overheard in the marketplace.
For you see it becomes you to be chastened:
for the old to envy the young,
and for youth to fear not getting older,
where the paths through the elms, the carnivals, begin.

And it was said of Gyges that his ring
attracted those who saw him not,
just as those who wandered through him were aware
only of a certain stillness, such as precedes an earache,
while lumberjacks in headbands came down to see what all the fuss
        was about,
whether it was something they could be part of
sans affront to self-esteem.
And those temple hyenas who had seen enough,

nostrils aflare, fur backing up in the breeze,
were no place you could count on
having taken a proverbial powder
as rifle butts received another notch.

I, meanwhile . . . I was going to say I had squandered spring
when summer came along and took it from me
like a terrier a lady has asked one to hold for a moment
while she adjusts her stocking in the mirror of a weighing machine.
But here it is winter, and wrong
to speak of other seasons as though they exist.
Time only has an agenda
in that wallet at his back, while we
who think we know where we are going unfazed
end up in brilliant woods, nourished more than we can know
by the unexpectedness of ice and stars
and crackling tears. We'll just have to make a go of it,
a run for it. And should the smell of baking cookies appease
one or the other of the olfactory senses, climb down
into this wagonload of prisoners.

The meter will be screamingly clear then,
the rhythms unbounced, for though we came
to life as to a school, we must leave it without graduating
even as an ominous wind puffs out the sails
of proud feluccas who don't know where they're headed,
only that a motion is etched there, shaking to be free.

Limited Liability

And one wants to know everything about everything.
Such is my decision, though I will abide by others,
that goes without saying. Still, I fell off the sandbar
walking back toward shore, and that was a time of sorrow,
even of great sorrow, for myself and many others.
No, make that a few others. Whatever I was
trying to do automatically broke the hearts
of those in the seats on either side of mine.
It was wild like weather, yet you couldn't just live in it,
you had to drool, your facial muscles had to twitch,
at least some of them. About the time the thought
of living in England occurs, and one succeeds in eating a
little asparagus and custard, the old guard revives its dug-in
positions. You knew about these. They were like lace and spring,
they went away but they never really did. They require a context
of mourning, and public relations. If a cock is being sucked
at a certain moment, it will not jiggle the seismograph, provoke regret
from one who is esteemed and dry, but rather break out disjunctedly
in another hemisphere, and people will start reasoning
from there on. The kid was only a gas-station attendant;
he couldn't have been more than seventeen or eighteen, yet the evening
wind begins promptly to blow, the morbid goddesses sing
that a brooch came undone and pricked one's finger, all silently:
so much for revanchisme. "But of course." And like it says here,
cooperation is part of the school of things, only don't get too close
to overboard, and be burned by the musing that sets in then.
Is that why cows live in clusters, why the foxglove
covers for the hay, and all gets done in a day like it was
supposed to, only there are no more feet to bathe?
I confess I was leery

the first time she told her story
but having heard it enough I can never get enough of what it was
    determined
should never be shielded from the rain or its attendant wetness;
by the same token they are always with us. Once I started
to count the ways I was indebted to the moose and its house
of night, some old saw had me battling again, kicking up moss
and letting it settle along with other debris. No
one saw me when I came here; I swear it. You can have a handle
on me now, only don't abuse it
too much yet. The sky popped out of the oven
like a tin of blueberry muffins, and there's so much to say.
Only I don't feel I'm dry enough. Yet. Take ten,
there's a good caddy. Go do someone's bidding,
then meet me under the larch when the storm crackles. I'll tell you
    then.

Love in Boots

Our first assignment was to make a square,
a place for living and carping in,
where the Sphinx could panhandle and maids desist,
if they cared to.

It seems my plan was too perfect!
People ended up hating it and the lives they lived in.
Back to the bogs! But the way was cut off,
or no one quite remembered it. *It should be here,*
somewhere . . .

In these demotic times one is grateful for a variety
of sundries: footprints on the prow of a ship,
or a wolf taking the trouble to cross over and tell you
he's engaged. Sunny things, the fins and buttons of childhood,

passing through grace and beyond it.
One finds there is time, after all, to wind the clock.
Yet no one noticed it had stopped. Would it make
the afternoon editions, blowing like mold across the blue
canyons we call our trellis, causing alembics to burst
in carnival sheds? What *about* next time? Could we eliminate it
from the list of essentials taxpayers pray for,
then shrink from, noticing it reflected in the rain barrel
when all the other dimensions remain quietly on hold?

Perhaps, on some more sophisticated planet,
these things tow the gravity they require,
and people are no match for them, don't even envy
or imagine them. Everything proceeds from a simple

gesture that never goes out of style. Yoo hoo. Look, it's Clara
and Amos. Aren't they simply divine? But it *is* getting late,

and I have to get up and chop wood tomorrow. Oh, if you're looking
for a timetable, it's there, in that train, that's now
two feet away, now one, but will never obstruct
or demolish us. Thank heaven for Zeno's paradox!

Love's Stratagem

The comparison says enough, really, nay is eloquent on the subject
of Paris furs, how she descended the avenue
wondering what was wrong, or warm. The best comparison
I can give you is two heads. His head literally exploded,
mine felt like a grape that prudent fingers leave on the bunch
to cloud over and legally pass out of the picture.

Yet his face it resembles a fig.
Where can I find seeds in heaven? I want to take some back to earth
    with me
and plant them if it's illegal. Imagine the surprised cackling!
My bedsores have healed! I just hit a hole in one!
My Labrador just had twins, and I don't know where to register them!
I replaced a file with a file

so asps wouldn't eat it. Now that we are out in the fun you must run
farther than any salmon bringing milt home to meet the missus.
Only say, if we are categorically united,
how many rooms does that make? Does one count the bathroom
or the patio, if it's enclosed? (*We'll have to make a run for it, don't
let on you know anything about Sheba.*) Er, where was I?

I know. I can see it now that the fog has evaporated
and taken most of the town with it. Come to think of it,
why did we settle here? Did God ordain it? Why couldn't we have
gone on just hanging around the window seat, head out the window,
eyes drooping, tongue lolling? Or were we meant to discover

the boiling point of Minnesota, the town in Nebraska?

Many Are Dissatisfied

yet the wind from Seattle blows over and over,
against the facing page and against the anthill.
You would wonder at all the crumbs
that have been dropped, lest you find your way
through this tangled story of ours,
and at how the gentlemen fliers cursed us
as mere entertainers, made us put our wallets away.

There was nothing they wouldn't do to make us comfortable,
short of approving our lifestyle.
Which is why I fester on the porch,
a Hun without a regiment, till the great pretender
comes to knock us over.
It was so gray and mild,
the evening we played air hockey, that I could hardly
condone your singing. You thought about your neighbor's come,
listlessly, as a child with a slinky badgers cardoons,
while in the great specialist's plaid-paneled waiting room
the air has gone mad.

My question to you now is: How
do we escape the fat boy, in lemon overalls,
twenty stories high, with feet two blocks in diameter?
I guess it was just that spring
emptied like an Egyptian sewer into the street,
fringing our losses before the bad time that went away.
Or is it all declamation—the wanting
to sue nature for the tide's infirmities,
sliding off into a lather,
mouthing the old pulchritude a house has?

Military Pastoral

Hello, Blubberface. You can come in now.
No, I didn't say *now*. What are you, My Man Godfrey?
Now go out and come in gently. What
had we asked you to bring? Or was it only
to show off reentering a different way?

In any case my apples are blasted.
This tin screen grates on my ear.
Asked back, over the tides and mangrove hummocks
of last year at this exact same time—
kind of makes you feel younger, doesn't it, buttocks,
if you're really in the mood for improvement?
But my pale army subsists on what it can scrounge
from the larders of thrifty *paysannes*.
All around me I see only hope and dopiness
etched against a sky of ferule tan, of so much incongruity
they fall slap in the middle of village streets.

And when I, vanguard of mortality, review my troops
it's as if the moisture had evaporated from the air.
I say one, two, twelve times. Only the thrush hears
and appreciates the humor of the saga, but of course
the cat already has its eye on her. We only learn from books,
I suppose, and partly hidden tattoos that tell of sunken treasure
and other boundless efforts that are required of no man.
Might as well unpack the laurels—they're starting to arrive.

My Name Is Dimitri

I am going to be your host tonight.
Do you wish the fiddle or the fish?
The hen with ivory sauce is very fine, very light.
An experience unlike any other pushes you

toward what holy extremities? To a margin of uncertainty
where not just drinks are muddled and an old frump
of a past straddles you. Uncertainty polishes the china
to a mirrorlike daze.

A World War I soldier wants to say Thank you,
Fuck you, from all the trenches his heart is bleeding
from, from the aghast question and the problem of novelty
to the tip of sores that ends this peninsula
back where it began, where the pilgrims trod.

There is so much in Warsaw—
too many restaurants, too few connections
that would otherwise make things interesting.
We have nothing to cling to, only torn memories

of a station between stations that wasn't
the one that was supposed to be there. An altar of roses
climbed halfway up the stadium which was full of misfits
with no store to come home to. Still, there was the bus,

a place beyond all others, curdled in the neat sky.
An insane child wishes the grass whipped less
at the bends where the posts are. The merger of innocents
matters less than the hum of interim authority and the screech of
    descants

that take you by surprise as they tide you over.
Goodnight. The windscreen is heavy with imagery
in entranced colors like the plumes of a canary
or lyrebird. Keep the rats out of that granary

and all will be well for a century, but if the mailman
leaves me no mail it will be a vast appointed mistake,
vast as a throne room in an old castle by the sea,
as Thuringia. The moss grew for me, and there
the matter rested, in salt pits and other geographical refuse.
Besides, they were coming over the ridge,
would save us, and then we'd see what we would see—
despondent daughters of the Hellespont, fickle as creation
and the lives that extend it down to this trough.

My Philosophy of Life

Just when I thought there wasn't room enough
for another thought in my head, I had this great idea—
call it a philosophy of life, if you will. Briefly,
it involved living the way philosophers live,
according to a set of principles. OK, but which ones?

That was the hardest part, I admit, but I had a
kind of dark foreknowledge of what it would be like.
Everything, from eating watermelon or going to the bathroom
or just standing on a subway platform, lost in thought
for a few minutes, or worrying about rain forests,
would be affected, or more precisely, inflected
by my new attitude. I wouldn't be preachy,
or worry about children and old people, except
in the general way prescribed by our clockwork universe.
Instead I'd sort of let things be what they are
while injecting them with the serum of the new moral climate
I thought I'd stumbled into, as a stranger
accidentally presses against a panel and a bookcase slides back,
revealing a winding staircase with greenish light
somewhere down below, and he automatically steps inside
and the bookcase slides shut, as is customary on such occasions.
At once a fragrance overwhelms him—not saffron, not lavender,
but something in between. He thinks of cushions, like the one
his uncle's Boston bull terrier used to lie on watching him
quizzically, pointed ear-tips folded over. And then the great rush
is on. Not a single idea emerges from it. It's enough
to disgust you with thought. But then you remember something
    William James
              .
wrote in some book of his you never read—it was fine, it had the
    fineness,

the powder of life dusted over it, by chance, of course, yet still looking
for evidence of fingerprints. Someone had handled it
even before he formulated it, though the thought was his and his alone.

It's fine, in summer, to visit the seashore.
There are lots of little trips to be made.
A grove of fledgling aspens welcomes the traveler. Nearby
are the public toilets where weary pilgrims have carved
their names and addresses, and perhaps messages as well,
messages to the world, as they sat
and thought about what they'd do after using the toilet
and washing their hands at the sink, prior to stepping out
into the open again. Had they been coaxed in by principles,
and were their words philosophy, of however crude a sort?
I confess I can move no farther along this train of thought—
something's blocking it. Something I'm
not big enough to see over. Or maybe I'm frankly scared.
What was the matter with how I acted before?
But maybe I can come up with a compromise—I'll let
things be what they are, sort of. In the autumn I'll put up jellies
and preserves, against the winter cold and futility,
and that will be a human thing, and intelligent as well.
I won't be embarrassed by my friends' dumb remarks,
or even my own, though admittedly that's the hardest part,
as when you are in a crowded theater and something you say
riles the spectator in front of you, who doesn't even like the idea
of two people near him talking together. Well he's
got to be flushed out so the hunters can have a crack at him—
this thing works both ways, you know. You can't always
be worrying about others and keeping track of yourself

at the same time. That would be abusive, and about as much fun as attending the wedding of two people you don't know.
Still, there's a lot of fun to be had in the gaps between ideas. That's what they're made for! Now I want you to go out there and enjoy yourself, and yes, enjoy your philosophy of life, too. They don't come along every day. Look out! There's a big one . . .

Nice Morning Blues

The promised "great getaway" turned out to be
shorter than anyone could have foretold. It was,
in its way, perfect. We looked down from a terrace
to the sea. Beneath its surface was another terrace,
and under that a different sea
of a color hitherto unimagined. And beneath that, the old campus
that had formerly stood there exhibited its perfection:
mitered slabs of stone in pale, meatlike tones
that put dentistry to shame.

How was I to know, leaving the garage,
that one of us would never meet the other again?
Yet round after round of schnapps was served
and that did seem to be a good thing.
There was an enormous choice of tempting salads—

And so it goes, visit followed visit
in a distressed but pristine season.
The crabapple blossoms were a deeper pink;
girls wore them on their skirts. There was always more
to do, with a promise of love in the evening.
And yes, nothing came of it. Nothing produced nothing.
We were saddest on the most luxurious perch,
or so it seems. Then sadness wanders away
like a child getting lost. What is there left to do?

No Earthly Reason

There are additional reasons having to do with security
for why we cannot extend to you this funding
unless you are prepared to keep an open mind,
fondle your pet discreetly.

"It has warm legs and a furry complexion," you said.

That's just fine. I keep my hat screwed to my head.
So, good. The pencil and pens in my pocket
that some make fun of are as lemon verbena to my ears.
If the tide-racked coasts rememorate it
no great moment attaches to it
(truth's medicine ball by itself)
but we want you to remain in this sanatorium,
out of harm's way, for at least a spell.

I could think of no earthly reason to give him my dress,
but I did it. He took it, walked off with it too.
And now the palms in the government palace courtyard
are busy filing their report. We're in it too—
about how many times I wash, how dreams come to me,
what brand of athletic shoes I buy. It makes me angry,
but my anger is as a doll is to a child:
insignificant in comparison to myself,
but occupying its secret corner anyway.

It would be nice if it was very dark
and only a little rent of light on the floor. I need your help.
Offer me sweet unguents. I'll tell you the same.

But in the parlor many floors below
the jury has already voted, using beans
kept for this purpose in a large glass canister.
We should know the verdict before long
he says coming closer his breath a fuzz on the sleeper's window.
It would be nice if a vulture could have some of this meat
but we have already tried justice in the streets.
It doesn't work. It would be better to run for your lives, and yet
I always linger. Behind a tree. I capture a great big bonus.

No Longer Very Clear

It is true that I can no longer remember very well
the time when we first began to know each other.
However, I do remember very well
the first time we met. You walked in sunlight,
holding a daisy. You said, "Children make unreliable witnesses."

Now, so long after that time,
I keep the spirit of it throbbing still.
The ideas are still the same, and they expand
to fill vast, antique cubes.

My daughter was reading one just the other day.
She said, "How like pellucid statues, Daddy. Or like a . . .
an engine."

In this house of blues the cold creeps stealthily upon us.
I do not dare to do what I fantasize doing.
With time the blue congeals into roomlike purple
that takes the shape of alcoves, landings. . .
Everything is like something else.
I should have waited before I learned this.

Obedience School

Let us leave the obedience school.
The door is open. Outside the sun is shining.
Why do you hesitate? Why do you hold back?

If there were some warts on the obedience school
we should have known about it before this.
You don't learn the cancan at obedience school.

Yup. But the parkway night is festering.
Besides, there are so many trained-dog acts now
nobody wants any competition.

That's why I bought Flossie the ticket
back to Puyallup. Her ladies-in-waiting
were flouting the scent of incense smoldering;

her high heels provoked "zounds!" of acclaim
from the wrong kind of gent-customer
we want no truck with.

And when the old school shudders
in a sudden ray of March sun,
accusers and behoovers alike will be believed;

behemoths and mammoths struggle and give up
in the aquarium dawn. Then a run on the feedstores
ensues. Causes are given up for lost. The queen's pony

capers on its hind legs, quite as if narcissism
were going out of style. Poor children! Why, it broke their heart,
but Dad's with them now. Dad can conquer this thing.

Ode to John Keats

From a dark land of figs
and morello cherries and plum jam
and lettered building blocks, the gold horn
extends its welcome to red paper fish.

The king has but one eye
but it is as round
as a dinner plate and sees
what others haven't the knack of,
except sages. Bursts of something
in midafternoon have flooded
the treasuries, roofed the spires
with stagnant dignity. One must
carry out these orders, or die
in the equation that links us.
Waiting for a bus requires more stamina,
or lurking under a weeping beech.

Of a Particular Stranger

My country is but scrubland,
plaguey country. From its opposite shore
I can see you sitting, surrounded by nursemaids
and rolled umbrellas. O it's not quitting
on us, my dear, only making a marginal note.
The time of tomes vast as valleys
hasn't approached us yet. Just wounded vets
doing the desert shuffle, a can of sperm
in one hand, a chilled beer in the other.

And I, I walk into the wrong room,
well-rounded, keeping my patience together.
A bat flies out over the tarmac.
We shouldn't have wasted so much hesitancy
on ourselves, it's for others, makes 'em feel genuine
and wanted. They start to like us,
then they *really* like us, it's too late
for them to cancel. They start to forget us,
then positively dislike us, as though we'd tampered
with their mnemonic machinery. An angel in brocade
witnesses this, copies it down.

By afternoon's end we were soaked
in a thrilling downpour that promised much
in the way of freshness, clamor. Writing, I
overshot the page into the sandtrap
of bucolic enthusiasm. You always rescue me
from such occasions, bind me to my own quiddity
and bookmarks. After all, there are a lot of books
to be read, lots of pages in this warehouse.

Operators Are Standing By

In some of the stores they sell a cheese rinse
for disturbed or depressed hair. You add whiskey
to it at the last moment. Now that
it's nearly Christmas, we could buy
such things, you and I, and take them with us,
though it seems like
only yesterday I hit that Halloween homerun.
It backed up and kind of flowed back
into my side I think, creating a "strawberry
jar" effect. There was nothing Arvin
or I could do about it.

Determining everyone is a bigshot
is sometimes all he cares about.
I've slept on the ground with him,
and deep in a birchbark canoe.
Once there was two of him.
At school no one could tell us apart
until we smiled, or his big laugh came unbuttoned.
Fatally, venery has taken its toll
of him these last years. I can't
get near him without being reminded of Venus,
or the hunt. I come in six different packages,
from the "jewel case" to Wrigley's spearmint.
In the time of friendly moose
droppings I followed them to the Shedd Aquarium.
No one was selling tickets that day.
I wandered in and out of the fish tanks,
stopping occasionally to leave a handprint
on the plate glass for the benefit of some fish or other.

Others Shied Away

The Autumn seems to cry for thee,
Best lover of the Autumn-days!
—SUSAN COOLIDGE

And they have cooler armchairs.
They have an imaginary tunnel down there.
It can be the color of your choosing. With bridges, splayed
so wide of the mark, you wonder how they thought of crossing.

It can't be over.
I haven't taken my final exam
nor received the notice
to do so. The halls for my oratory
haven't been built yet. They'll be nice and new,
with buff-colored dolphins dangling from the ceiling.
The world will see something of my art in this,
though I had nothing to do with the actual building, and turn away,
admiring me and their clothes—so appropriate!
How did we know how the moon was going to be today,
what drinks to serve after driving fifty miles through parched savannas?
Yet does it all come miraculously to life?
Or is it the solitary crank who's right,
the unofficial historian? He never hazards an opinion,
yet stays by the door like a porter, pose
that fools no one. It seems none of us has begun to digest
the meal of all our lives. There's nothing left to do but count the
      rooms—
nine, all told.

I told you when I set out for
the market town, the saddlebags would be full
of gold and silver coinage, just for you;

coffers would bulge, orchards
overflow their walls with blue fruit.
Every day would be a cocktail party, all day long.
Now the tunnel seems withered.
We must return to the sparse blessings
that place our shoes on this winter path;
nothing can stay outdoors all the time—
there must be intervals for books and fire
and endless conversation that means very little
unless we'd prefer to have it some other way,
little girl, blinking at the autumn's rough practice,
crude language, distemper—wound into a ball for you.

Palindrome

In the days of French film and infanticide
and red flannel hash, words we kept for trading
up, which were later lost, other lost words,
angry at being snubbed for so many years,
surrounded us like owls in a boathouse. "To whom
are we indebted for the honorable occasion?" Words
no dictionary ever knew, or acknowledged having known,
like "spludge" or "parentitis." But then, what can we do,
there are so many, like zillions of bats
emerging from a cave at sunset, feeling the cool air
thread deliciously down their membranes. Yet they too
can get us in trouble. And it's fun to play along,
ears cocked for no special din, until the thud
of morning commences, and a child appears,
etched on the air of my room.

Penthesilea

No more odes, the good doctor said.
Come in with something distressing. Aw,
we said, the silted lakes are obedient already.
That is to say, a run on cash at the banks
that will never be mismatched or compensated.

The nice person sat and drank tea. You know
how it is when you find a café space
that is yours ideally, that snakes eternally
past a bit of ecstatic burnt blue from the street
around the corner. A place where nettles lean enthusiastically
like acrobats or stoats. O much as we
love you you can't come in.

But I did something before I died,
like bringing the wind into the house with the wood,
making it sit far off over there, in the thin corner.
The red furniture grew up.
Suddenly it was the rush hour, and we were on our hands and knees
trying to find the magnifying glass
that speaks in measured terms of these deliria,
and tying on one's skates,
half a century from the grouches of home.

Plain as Day

with all its accoutrements
(of course)—intact, impervious
to air, sand, and time—the three fatal
sisters with nary a thought
in their heads except where to cut it—
and it goes out, like a candle or a father
to buy a pack of cigarettes. You knew
this. WE all knew it. It's the old

weather shuffle behind a different
sun veil—shot, diapered
the way they always want it.

It never snows on Tuesday—far
be it from me to suggest otherwise, only
there *is* this difference, this little difference
that won't go away,
that's been waiting since before the office opened.
What shall I tell it?

Those that are taken leave no footprint
on the air, no smile
on the soused sky.
It's another kind of smile
speeding toward us like an express train
we'll never see. Please put out the light,
the ashes, when you leave.

Same in Texas or Louisiana. Meaning
no mail for you today, and would you please call back?

It's urgent. Well, *was*. I've been waiting hours
on a bench next to a fugitive general.

"Be sure of retail," he says. "The life insurance
building, the pickle garden. Heaven knows they
attack our radar too, swoop down on us like bats
and the mystery illness."

Are you Big Bang?

Point Lookout

The object of the game is, after all, not to die but to grow into easeful
death, winning. Forty shopkeepers sinned and for this they were
    betrayed.

He seems not to have understood the rules of perspective.

We have the technology to tame the edges.
For this we must become hedgehogs again, blindly entertaining all the
philosophy of light.
It goes nice and easy like a drink, or remark in a salon.
All this time we were wishing, we
wished to hazard an accomplishment or two.
Come, I'll play you an old comedy
of the bartered bear and soothsayer, no ways to be out of doors, no
thing on the milky plain, the wind dropped. Soft
from my curlicue she bounces around.
The animal traces hovered and steamed. The soft shell of a particle
twists itself off from the name, stands defiant, budged.

We mourn those who do briefly paddle.

Poor Knights of Windsor

Say it was any day.
A knock on the door, a neoclassic cannonball flies past.
The hall is done up in scarlet; something more powerful
than just plain good taste is obviously at work here.

I agree to share your game with you.
We saunter on the terrace (Emerson
said a man should "saunter"). We eat some trail mix.
Gosh, what a limited bunch of things to do there is.

Anything that can be done with stale bread
will sometime be done. The English like to
twist it and dip it in something till it hardens: the result
is called "Poor Knights of Windsor."
It's some kind of savory.

They don't have those much anymore,
and we, why we never had them.
That applies to most things. Not plumbing, though—
if anything we have too much of that.

But those knights,
having to stand by a checkered cloth, pretending
it was OK by them, this really not much more than a scrap,
like the rarebit the hunter's wife tosses him when he comes home late,
his game bag empty
his fun exhausted
ready for a round of Monopoly—

Does the heraldry impose itself,
trickling on the forehead

for all to see?
Do brands ultimately matter?
Are the lasses more froward? The lads
bent over backward? What is this thing
you wanted me to see? Oh, a shovel. You might have said so.
And the way back is polluted, the spears
almost indecent.

Quick Question

We took to the lake
in small boats.
The once-in-a-lifetime flood
was approaching on dainty, centipede legs.
Something about the gestalt
told me not to release this comment to the wire services
before the various motivations were rehashed.

This was the next day.
Only a few empty cans met the gaze.
"Sprinkle it!" the children advised.
"Oil quickly becomes rancid."
Matter of taste, he thought.
Or matter of boobs.

Sometimes an old woman is coming to get you
through the boughs that were her home.
It's enough if the summer night light
can chasten, the tree-barbs sustain you
on their perjured breath.
There's no returning to haggle,
then. The sea is like pale green linoleum
and all the grenadiers have returned to Sicily.

Detraining, one thinks: This house was always haunted
by porcupines, which is as it should be.
Waiting for people to get down to business,
put their cards on the table, can be such a random act, like a minuet
of gnats against a blistered sky.
That is something to stare at: neither squat,

nor a tenement. A block of some often-penetrated material,
a liquid of another density, crawling along like honey
to greet its forebears—

better to leave ribbons of sand behind.
The journey becomes you, but is its way of becoming,
valid until the gold pinprick
comes to a head further along further night?
Shall we embark tomorrow,
when a favorable wind rustles the sheets?

Reverie and Caprice

It seems very unlikely that my wishes will
be accomplished "in the name of the Lord."
Couldn't He have foreseen this? What is this?
Tragic mealtime preparations
beneath a paper-bag colored sun that wants
to cast no light. And pockets
or strips of difference, fresh from the paper shredder.
How much cleaner would it be now,
O my works, if to be left alone
had been the original thrust, not this
woven screen, like wicker or billowing fabric,
tense but loosely dwelling
in the hostile night from which we took directions.

And after we climbed
a certain distance it was only a boy
in a suit with his bird. Unidentified youths
set off after him and were never seen again.
The banyan tree loomed large, and nothing came of it,
only a preposterous jelly made of shards
of boiled facts and unkept promises. Promises
that were never intended to be kept—she had a saying:
"Never stay in the pantry
while the mill is operating." Pure, putrescent poetry.
All along you were trying to make me give up the other.

Safe Conduct

The coast is clear. Bring me my scallop shell of quiet,
my spear of burning gold. I am definitely setting out tonight,
unless someone calls, to immerse myself in the Great Lore,
which I should have been doing all along. Never mind,
it can wait, it's been around long enough. I am afraid
it might involve cutting a swath through the fruited jungle.

That was the other thing about him: how many times
he avoided using the word "eclipse." It was as though
he bore his personal darkness with him, furled
like an umbrella, but ready to snap to attention
at the fall of a wombat's tear. It would be sufficient

to engulf us for centuries, thanks. The innocence
of his position, as laid out by him, before God and the elders,
drew delighted applause from the sparse crowd at the racetrack.
"And if we come home with you tonight," one beribboned lady caroled,
"will you tell us about Midas and the seltzer bottle? Pretty please?"

I am annoyed before each investigation
that will definitively clear my name. A toad watches me
from a lily pad, its lidded eyes plunged in despair.
"Was it for this I tamed you, brought you up from mere pollywog
to outstanding frog prince? Alas, the mists
that gather now are of the old kind, from the Iron Age,
and every instrument you practiced then
is being fine-tuned for tonight's one-person recital."

Salon de Thé

Some time before you wore that belt
on a boat, with a tree branch covering half the Caucasus,
I asked if she knew the *Caucasian Sketches*
of Ippolitov-Ivanov—"It's like looking at a distant aviary."
Yes, and the chords are like bullets
that can reach halfway to Siberia.
Very committed they are, and faithful
to their idea of the troops.

The troops need no notion
but a path through the rocks always helps,
like dessert and laundry. Oh, if you were going to change your shirt,
but I like this one. It's time to buy a new one.
Does my lemon-zest-patterned tie please you? Oh, I implore you,
no talking on the phone after 9 p.m.

Then the ladies got busy,
hung rugs on the metal clothesline and walloped them,
a good afternoon. Your sister was waiting on the shore
to tell me it was time to get to my job as busboy
at the Cloak and Dagger Tearoom. Makes me squeamish
just to imagine it. And it *was* a hard time,
but in summer, at least, you could dress cheaply
and look just like the rich kids
in their darkened limos.

I'll hear no more about it.
The bank messenger wants Fuzzy to stay away from me,
and all along I thought we were playing for apples,
but the reward money came as gourds, plastic-colored ones.
The kittens showed some restraint
and the shade was lowered as it is every Doomsday.

See How You Like My Shoes

Two twisted dry turds on the sidewalk;
the weather one's gray dropcloth.
What town is this?
The weather has a choke hold on foreseeing
what happens to it.
Heck there is nothing but the alike
except persons are not. Things are
like institutions. Stumbling from perjured
personhood, all seem alike
but the fugitive person has got things
his sisters (in Olympic
statehood) haven't got: to mimic
two legs like a dog is out
and times three sheet music in the door
is to planting. They really resist,
soaringly. The salesman head
is two whole shoes, and that be
the graveyard by the flame talking,
earnest ouch spelled by night.

The great symphony fell down before it could be revived.
On this oceloted tree they still think and wonder
how the person caved in
yet remained so spick-and-span a presence
all during the end-of-century doldrums
someone forgot in the telling.
They was many of same left out.
Many felt left out
their beat repealing to the besotted orbs
left out in the rain. Yet I am this person,
you. I like to titter.

Sleepers Awake

Cervantes was asleep when he wrote *Don Quixote*.

Joyce slept during the Wandering Rocks section of *Ulysses*.

Homer nodded and occasionally slept during the greater part of the
    Iliad; he was awake however when he wrote the *Odyssey*.

Proust snored his way through *The Captive*, as have legions of his
    readers after him.

Melville was asleep at the wheel for much of *Moby Dick*.

Fitzgerald slept through *Tender Is the Night*, which is perhaps not so
    surprising,

but the fact that Mann slumbered on the very slopes of *The Magic
    Mountain* is quite extraordinary—that he wrote it, even more so.

Kafka, of course, never slept, even while not writing or on bank holidays.

No one knows too much about George Eliot's writing habits—my guess
    is she would sleep a few minutes, wake up and write something,
    then pop back to sleep again.

Lew Wallace's forty winks came, incredibly, during the chariot race
    in *Ben Hur*.

Emily Dickinson slept on her cold, narrow bed in Amherst.

When she awoke there would be a new poem inscribed by Jack Frost
    on the windowpane; outside, glass foliage chimed.

Good old Walt snored as he wrote and, like so many of us, insisted he
    didn't.

Maugham snored on the Riviera.

Agatha Christie slept daintily, as a woman sleeps, which is why her
    novels are like tea sandwiches—artistic, for the most part.

I sleep when I cannot avoid it; my writing and sleeping are constantly
    improving.

I have other things to say, but shall not detain you much.

Never go out in a boat with an author—they cannot tell when they are
    over water.

Birds make poor role models.

A philosopher should be shown the door, but don't, under any circumstances, try it.

Slaves make good servants.

Brushing the teeth may not always improve the appearance.

Store clean rags in old pillow cases.

Feed a dog only when he barks.

Flush tea leaves down the toilet, coffee grounds down the sink.

Beware of anonymous letters—you may have written them, in a wordless implosion of sleep.

Something Too Chinese

for me now.
And I thought how strange, one is always
crying after this and that,
against all odds.

As in the sex game, shimmering
like a peach—the *impératrice*
measures your guns, the townspeople
shuffle around, the one who will be the hero
is still viper-thin, and green
as hope. We all need a change of scene,
she said, a change of air—

try the sea. It is good for some persons.
A closet works best for me
with a view of an abandoned apple tree,
a wedge of porch. *Here, take these*—
running with the hare, I'll be back instanter,
before you can observe you, wipe the grime
and tears from the mirrored clock
over and against time.
These are mere cavils.

Swaying, the Apt Traveler
Exited My House

It's so easy to be attractive when
you're young, even if not particularly favored by nature,
even if nerdy, spotted, and pacific,
even in the wrong clothes, rumpled with anxiety
like a maze, even if without interests
from the wrong side of the street.

Standing with one's bother,
wiping off the strictures of dark, demented doubt,
one believes what one lives in.
The air freshens the rooms.

I float from the dormer down
to the brick path darkened by the lawn sprinkler.
It seems I was inside once.

Oh I'm careless to tell the advantage of that pact
with truth I made as I undress.
The truth is it would have gotten to me
after five or six seasons of that sort of thing.
But it wasn't to be. Baby blushed anew at the air's demands,
and the pine tree fell over on the back porch, causing it to cave in.
That wasn't in my list of grievances though.
In fact there was never any list;
I coped by coping, living out life shred by shred
until a magma caught up with me. In the broken alley
one passed strollers and people pushing them. One comet caught my
      eye
but it was too late, too late to praise she always says.
My pants were wet

and someone is coming up the road, some zombie
or other.
This tune I never asked for
is a different one, a furious clarion
shrilling a hornet's nest of replies.
The others will be older, other rapists
than the ones that were put down.

It would be time to plan an escape.
This is difficult in a hotel.
There are bands of bullies waiting to frisk
you, and on the esplanade the scenario doesn't get much better:
Even the little girl with the balloon is planning to annex half of
    Western civilization,
and the ticket-of-leave man has his eye on the colored bastions
we plummet over, seeking release in the sea, the sea!
Two dolphins like two colons in a sentence
are rinsing me now,
pouring me out from myself.
I feel as though I'll never be big enough
to efface scars as an adult ideally should—
wait, though! I'm coming to the corner where
pockets of jasmine and lavender inhale—
Be my scope limited, it's something
just to have been in the intimacy of all the stories
down the stairway to where it ends, to have worn
linen and passed as a man in suits.
I'll tell that one too
though you don't want to hear it,
though it's as old as the hills,

though displeasure is now rage, I'll canvass
for funds for it, not giving up,
not showing myself up this time,
too close to Mother and the difficult calm,
to the overextended fruit of this day,
this dream.

Taxi in the Glen

You throw matches on the floor.
I collect antique lard cans.

"You know, some day there'll be an interest
in these, though it will peak, like the tide,
in infinite relief, and be back next day.
But somebody will surely remember them—
the succinct red of that metal.
Then we drink everything in, avidly,
yet we are not thirsty. Some mechanism declines
our auroras, and so must it even be
until the day of waking up and not finding out.
I'll be a spruce-god by then, but you, you
should still be savoring the advantages
of belated puberty."
                    And I'll dress you in grass
and sing to you, a song where the words are the music
and the music has no point. Let me chafe your nipple, I . . .

And time will be happy. *Quiet, runt.*
The world's most astonishing plant couldn't
faze you, nor the fat ogres beyond the icehouse.
Lilies and sweet peas think you're swell.
I even have a nephew who is about
to invite you to the cotillion in Baltimore,
after taking a few more readings, and say,
wasn't it cool the way the alive came up to you,
all combustible, dreadful with tears,
and capped your burning oil well?

You've got friends
out there, more than you know,
but time is running short and we have to do something about it.
How about a nice whistle, something Grandma
can use on her back porch. Or a subscription
to *Reader's Digest* and the black methane-haunted city.
In any case it will be a peaceful interlude
when you get around to it—limning storm clouds
with the rigor one knows of old
of you—and caution an angered bluebottle
to calm his romantic hopes.

The Blot People

Something's not right. There were vibrations,
"vibes," a moment ago. A bush rubbed its bark against the sky.
The miserable thicket smelt of firecrackers

and I found everything in more or less the same order
when I got home. Still, it's hard to remember
what the order was after the first few things: a tie, a sofa,
a sheet of paper artfully placed so as to point to
who might have moved it in my ripe absence:
the bruised, alien thing, but familiar
as a smile on the face of anyone.

A few coat hangers jingled slightly
in the breeze from the closet. Someone was here.
Someone may triumph over the other one.
The family returns from the sea
with dogs and radios and fishing rods.
Old fishermen greet them in the ruddy glow
of lamps. The prisoner, an Uncle Joe,
returns after a great distance—so many miles,
so many hours tethered into days
that built the long log road from here to the east.

The Captive Sense

Nothing I'd ever want to own,
this feudal inequity transmits
its haze through the computer's
silent convulsions.

I'd wager there's life in the old bird yet—
the château of shaving cream is the most refreshing
thing to come along since tires in the theater.
When I arrive in the morning can I send it
collect, on the half shell? No? Not my fault?

I'm not going to tell you about regularity and anything,
me, Moses on my little raft. When it comes time
to rescue me, they will. Even four thousand years are
"like an evening gone." Some prosperity spurts
from its core, the core of waiting.
How could it be otherwise? Colored fountains in the night,
playing to dulcimers who dream of crocodiles?

My wish kept me captive, growing in it
till I fitted it exactly. And now the soothsayers can take over.

The movie dream was corny anyway, something
with spear carriers and a woman spinning flax
in a hovel by the sea, how great waves carried her along
to this pleasant plateau we are pleased to think of as
the present, conniving with something eldritch behind there
that takes me back. Never knew my heart could be so yearny.

From Hollyhock House to the Hollywood Hotel
the ill-lit Undine evolves, sashays even.

Who could have known the future would be such a big bunch,
and our share in it so meticulously outlined?
Not fiends, surely. But not friends, either.

The Confronters

Which of the incredible lies will prove true?
Ah, you ask me things
I wish I could not even ask myself.

A fire burns in a fireplace.
Cups are on a sill.

A man is working. He moves along. There is so
much to learn, so many teachers.

A dog howls from a roof.
Is it a wolf? Someone wants it to be.

In short there are these topics.
In winter and in summer there were.
The other seasons mediate
and end up having more topics.

"Hives with no bees," you said.
Which is how I remember them
through a bloodred transparent curtain, that looked
like rubber.

The various inequalities are parceled out,
now. There are suburban subdivisions
with no shards of land left on them.
Impatient dawns arrive.

The Desolate Beauty Parlor

on Beach Avenue

So much has impaired here
as well as getting here. It's where
we used to trade personals, then divide up
the aptly named "spoils." You know the kind of crud
I mean. Zombie set-tos,
the kind of thing.

It was impossible to locate hell or heaven
standing in the basement, inspecting
which pipes might have led to upstairs.
And the little pines off the street—
so sweet, but no sweeter
than what's been taken down in the interim.
I wonder where people hang their laundry nowadays,
who's for sale.

Then I saw it over Cannibal Beach—
a big baboon of a moon wafting this way
and that across the silken heather. It gave me
the widdershins. I'm still counting.
But the nice octagon trainer—*he* offered something
in the way of comfort, that eyeglasses can choose to go
and fit if they're so inclined. I'm talking
product now, and the new productivity
that comes from it. No one can afford
to ignore it anymore. Sure, sheep
bawl at their station, mad at having voted,
at being voided. But another way of sexy being
has been unveiled, and disturbed. I almost think
they won't be able to fix it, but it's so new—

Wait for the end, though. It's a small, arched close
built to contain ragged passions, and emptied
of them at present. The dale sweeps down
the sober dawn. Every face shows signs
of extreme concentration. Now *that's*
the way I'd like to behold you. For always.
For when the clipper blows astray and the
cheap shot is parted.

The Faint of Heart

were always right
about things like chansons de geste
and why they couldn't, at the time, be bothered.
Huon de Bordeaux was a highly important person
at least in Bordeaux which is an important French city,
that smells better than Perth Amboy but worse than Newton-le-
    Willows.
As has been pointed out
by myself and by other researchers, the object of the game
is to sit on a cold rattle.

I love the broad avenues of Washington, D.C.,
all leading toward—what? What is it they are escaping from?
Who in this great city cares anything about these data
that are the wellspring of truth? Torches emblazon the field
in front of the White House, which is where our president sits,
and Congress, when it is in session. Have I omitted anybody?
No, only the man who summons the president's taxi
who is too unimportant to figure in your list.
What about that dray horse's withers? Ah,
I shall have to begin again,
to start all over again from the beginning. Nomenclature
being its own reward.

And the fang? It's pleasant-looking and practical.
The board of surveyors is ours.
I trust in and admire it.
The Bureau of Mines belongs to all of us
in this dang-blasted country. Each of us has a share in tomorrow.
The light on that ilex

reminds me of an old school-chum of mine. None of us,
you see, was ever divested of anything,
which is why we're running riot now, in the alphabet-coded streets
and others named in memory of hydrangeas and vernal blushes.
And he said, "Varnish the floor!"
Winter is coming and it's going to be spectacular.
The squirrels and woolly caterpillars told me so.

In time the review squads appeared.
They carried Gatlings and were dressed in plum-colored eighteenth-
        century uniforms.
The mood was sour. I offered to chase a member of the enemy
but it wasn't going down well. Then *you* appeared, covered
with rubies, and it was decided we should "get down."
Secaucus had looked better. The snow on the reeds—

Soon the president joined us. He was worried but polite.
The daughters in their simple white frocks came out on the White
        House lawn
and had a very nice chat. They said it was an allegory
or oligarchy, and to roll with the punches. Better
alive and upbraided than rocked in the cradle of the deep,
someone said. But that's what I'm trying to oppose—
how you been?

The Green Mummies

Avuncular and teeming, the kind luggage
hosed down the original site. Who is ready
last, but I kind of get a kick
out of what-the-heck's surface optimism.
He doesn't believe in sex—that's *one* point
in his favor—but knows all the standard
Antonio stories and has told them to the Ladies'
Auxiliary in Loophole. You see, all his life
he wanted to be a trainer, or *something*, maggots
even. But fate's crow-like wing
had other plans for him. We were meant to have slept
during the time we were awake and learning; conversely,
as air-raid wardens we made good Michelin men—the tummy
always in repose, the chin barely protected by a ruff
of sneering blight. But it's time

you took that old comforter off. Adam and Eve
on a raft could say good day here, laughter in the
loved opus sounding. Yet wan derision only
watches, won't come forward. Next year is electric;
this one only divides and serves us, bathes us,
as we know how. Better pickled moray
than a jungle diorama, full of who-knows-what quirks
and surfaces. Yet I like him; his white hat
fell off and landed in the sound. Mortified,
he herded us into the vestibule; we had brought
the wrong kind of medlars.

The Latvian

Knowing John, it might have been.
Then again, maybe *you* know him—
food on his dried-up puss,
handsome for a day, a stunning
figure.

Why any of this bothers me, *I'll* never
know. My place is down here, with you
pagans and sun-worshippers, to whom
we turn when all else is exhausted, as, in fact,
it usually is. Then smiles break out
on rain-stippled streets, plaid plastic hats
and flowers appear. It's enough
to put the "cow" back in "macabre."

And we weave together the lesson
of today, me holding the ball of yarn,
you at your embroidery hoop.
Relief comes on strong. It pits
man against ghost, neighbor to neighbor,
falling down as the fur flies.

Who knew if the embassy had tickets,
or if they would even sell one?
By that time it was half past nine:
too late to dust the refrigerated air,
too early for the hockey scores.
Yet if I infiltrate this page of music,
like a violinist inflating Mozart, the seams,
the dear themes, come true.
We are all a falling in love.
Let's leave it that way.

The Military Base

Now, in summer, the handiwork of spring
is all around us. What did we think those
tendrils were for, except to go on growing
some more, and then collapse, totally
disinterested. "Uninterested" is probably
what I should say, but they seem to like it here.
At any rate, their secret says so,
like a B-flat clarinet under the arches
of some grove.

The house took a direct hit
but it didn't matter; the next moment
it was intact, though transparent.
No injuries were reported.
There were no reports of looting
or insane buggery behind altars.

The Peace Plan

These are the eyes I have stared out—
the others' suit them. Not to cry,
though. I brought the wind
and a pharmacist with me. You know, nuts and bolts.

Once on Lake Ontario
the swan heaped up her cries, the wind then
knew what to do, came in at a right angle,
the lake stoppered, parceled, traduced made it all seem plainer
as plain things can seem.

Then a licensed party might be drawn
she thinks. The horse, sheepish in his manger, shifts
from foot to foot—when was I last shod?
Will all these old differences unmake me at last,
or do I have to wait for a peach to blow?

A white-headed sage
remarks your angst, walks on
to the corner of Tilsit and Mulberry
whence he is abruptly inducted into heaven.

To what uncheer
has this oasis brought us?
Have some pagan robbers bought us
without our knowing? Then stealth
will be my cry, season after season, even
as the virgins on the porch circle round, take up a collection
of obliging smiles.

The Penitent

What are these apples doing here?
I thought I told you never to bring them inside.

And that wedding cake—what does it think it is?
Promises? Was it for this I sublet the apartment,

consecrated myself to a life of prudery
and banal satisfaction? I could have sold my life

story to a famous writer. But by then
it would have been over. Too much to write about isn't a good thing.

He recognized me! The famous man
knew my name! He held my hand

a second. I'd do that for someone.
The library is too fast tonight,

there's some spoilage in the lagoon, but everyone
is looking forward to your coming of age,

to the diamond stickpin and the hat.
Yet others carp,

seek annoyance, complain of the shadow,
as though 'twere always dusky night,

but your face looks good in the bathroom mirror.
I like your air freshener, your after-shave—

Say, what is it you do to look and smell so good?
Methinks some of it might come off on me

in the forest, with the cool sky
ambient with rubbings.

The Problem of Anxiety

Fifty years have passed
since I started living in those dark towns
I was telling you about.
Well, not much has changed. I still can't figure out
how to get from the post office to the swings in the park.
Apple trees blossom in the cold, not from conviction,
and my hair is the color of dandelion fluff.

Suppose this poem were about you—would *you*
put in the things I've carefully left out:
descriptions of pain, and sex, and how shiftily
people behave toward each other? Naw, that's
all in some book it seems. For you
I've saved the descriptions of chicken sandwiches,
and the glass eye that stares at me in amazement
from the bronze mantel, and will never be appeased.

The Sea

We carry our anxiety about the land with us
when we leave the land to travel overseas.
She shouts: "This is the dimmest
thing you ever did! In all time
was never such lurching, so much rubbing of the chin."

It's true: I'd have deserted the land of my forefathers
a dozen times before if I'd thought
I could get away with it.
And a triangular shadow whose apex is my toe
comes to tell me of my rights, warning me
of perjury, in some books the most serious crime of all.

Even the crinkled stars in the meadow
cannot look the other way, forcing me
into my constrained idea of myself.
I must go out with the light, and some day
someone will see through and love me.
I look down at these asters, unsteady,
unsure of what to grab. The tuneless sing to me.

The Shocker

What would I learn? That this vale
of sudden diphtheria matters less than a string.
That nudism equals terror.

My universities, you let me graduate
into a world riddled with solemn put-puts,
echoing across a bay in south Jersey,
fresh from delivering funnel cakes, a local specialty.
The brambles of the surf tangle
with the rafters of the beach. The Sea of Tranquillity.
You'll always get a kind of hum. No use
doffing those earmuffs. Besides it's not cold enough
to be wearing them. Amazed
people will look at you like you're crazed.
Now, all I wanted was to be back at the table
in my little laboratory, observing water spots on a plate,
trying to tune the old crystal set
to KDKA.

Here the weather is tethered to no air.
The eyes in the head in the house
look out over a spotty landscape of bilious green chest hair.
I believe I am the Man from Nowhere. I'm expected.
The taxi karma circled the pebbled drive and departed
through the great iron gates, which clanged shut.
You see I have to stay here. I *am* expected.
Yes well we'll pursue that over cocktails
and lunch.

They were destined to meet one more time.
briefly. Is that a hand on my sleeve . . .

The Waiting Ceremony

The binding clause—
it concerns us,
behooves us to behoove it.
Yet I'm so far away
(I'm not far away) . . .

Eighty-eight keys on a piano—
how do they know that?
I mean, *know* that? Oh, sure,
I know how they know it.
Excuse me for living.

Once in a while
the fun gets taken out
of what wasn't supposed to be fun.
That's the boiling point, what
they mean by one.

I get a stiff neck watching.
But then it seems old cereals (or serials)
are the part-time joke—like this rubber of bridge,
with all the bridges receding into the distance, brought
to their time of rightness. I would stress
the very white side of a house. Go on,
give it away, give it to a child
or some tax-free person.
(Nothing bumptious about that.)

We hold all the ends
of the story, like the four corners of a sheet,
resuming and resuming. We are the thick.
And the thin.

The Walkways

To know how to walk in the night, to have
a goal, to reach it in the darkness, the shadows.
—JOUBERT

The man behind you spoke to the tracery
as it killed him. The witches' envoy
brought a tusk to the guest of honor.
It was covered with vapid inscriptions about not
exhuming the past until the day
when smoke rises from a hole in the ground
alarming no tots, but then a journey like a cipher
elaborates its undoing. To have knitted scarlet
earnests in the epistolary novel of my Russian phrase book
and cloned them to a besmirched integrity
was my plan all along. There was no need to get your
balls in an uproar. Now, during one of the violinist's durable
encores the horse is teed off again, galloping toward the horizon
with the frail buggy and its precious cargo (two terrified
jeunes filles) in tow; the violet ribbon comes undone
and precious antique letters pepper the landscape
of early spring with plangent, mourning-dove complaints.

Why did you never write me? I bled for centuries
from that tiny puncture wound. One day I woke up whole
and it was all unreal, though I could hear the music
of your fingertips sliding over vellum, the scenery.
Meanwhile I had been getting stronger every day
without anyone's suspecting it, myself least of all.
When I finally stood up my head towered above the hills
and brass gates, terrorizing the little folk
beneath, who raced like ants in all directions.
Now I was past caring. Those feverish gifts

from many Christmases ago ceased to implore
or annoy. I eyed them wanly. Only a picture of a barefoot girl
sitting on a fence rang a distant bell, and that sullenly,
too deeply buried in today's growth
to answer my clear call.

I understand by this that you are taking over.
Wait—here is the key. Now that Lord Chesterfield has joined us
you'll need it to unlock conversations, great ones,
as a great wind is great. I am lucky to have come so far, only so far,
though the pantheon receives us all. Such is its way.
To be roofed and slavish, and then unstitched by apes,
is all a fellow needs, these modern days, unkempt, mourning
beside a gate, forever undecided,
like a partially opened umbrella.

The Water Carrier

I did not, then,
or later, pull my finger out of the hole
and make us as comfortable as possible.

While driving down East Raven Street
baroque and proud,
extend my hand to the nearest of you,
only the nearest.

Our decisions were made in filing-card days.
Now, someone else emotes.
Was it—? The oh-so-long summer,
gravel in one's boots—then, at night,
lettuces.

But continuing along
then, as now, soul-kissed
the powers, one after the other
into a haunting new day.

By the dried-out concrete pier
another was watching,
slowly, spilling his beans
into the pants, or porridge, of the night thing.

Then there were only a few of us orphans
who laugh, and shout,
lingering by the manure pile

who do daylong things.

Theme

If I were a piano shawl
a porch on someone's house
flooding the suave timbre . . .

Then forty, he,
a unique monsieur—
and yet he never wanted to look into it.

"Have you forgotten your little Kiki?"
Smoke from the horses' nostrils
wreathed the pump by the well.

The stink of snow
was everywhere. Too bad it looks
so good.

O beautiful and true
thou that glitterest
, in storms,

starting to discuss gardening. I don't
want to throw cold water
on this.

That music has changed my life
a lot, since I made the
mistake of learning it.

Another passionless day. The peach
forms a stain
at the end of the line.

Learn to lock love enjoy:
"The dream I dreamed
was not denied me;

hence my love is mad—
a castle's satin walls
folded in blood."

The deputy returned
the peashooter. I have learned
to plait wasps

into a bronze necropolis.
The ticket and the water
only endure, as one can

in the right circumstances,
mon cher Tommy. I think the theme
created itself somewhere

around here and cannot find itself.

Three Dusks

I think it's nice of me
to admire this coastline
of small houses:

firm outlines.
How the drainpipes sag
in the eves,

reserved for the bounciest
critter.

Ouch! Was that a new flavor?

    •

Anyway, they come and go.
No point in trying to stop 'em
or say hello: They'd misinterpret
this as a sign of greed
on your part. I know;
that's why I ripped up the goalposts.

    •

No one ought to know
what I was thought to know
for many years, among cherries
and without. The victor wears a stovepipe hat.

Your mucilaginous narratives come from somewhere:
I *know* that. I urge you to use your influence

with the young prince. He's headstrong,
and a bit difficult, besides, at times.
You're a perfect size 7,
you know. Yes, I know.

But what comes out of me
strolls back into dark.
It were not good
to show much of me,
only what red
neon can understand,
whisper to a little brother.

There were tens of thousands of cabbages
in the field.
Now, what one wanted was a little broth
with butter in it.

The cranes have flown far from their perch . . .

Today's Academicians

Again, what forces the critic to bury his
agenda in interleaving textualities and so
bring the past face-to-face with his present
isn't naughty, but it *is* both silly and wrong.
The past will have to get by on sheer pluck
or charm, entirely consistent with its ten-
dency to nullify and romanticize things. The
way a pain begins. The flying squirrels of
this particular rain forest mope in flight;
the audience has already done what it can for
them; and the pure light of their endeavor
bespeaks the modesty of the program: "mere?"
anarchy. That the men with spotted suits
and ties get down to it is one more nail in
their coffin. These portly curmudgeons dig-
nify no endeavor and are also about as "right"
as the weather ever gets. All in my time.
More meteor magic. Seems like.

Touching, the Similarities

Surely it was the same blank wall of twenty years ago.
How the past identified with every kind of collectible,
so there were not just the things we knew about.
The girl in white ran across the little bridge scattering pigeons
this way and that, there was no contenting them.
A little house poked up from under the vines.

Have a few beers at the Topple Inn,
throw a few darts at the board, put
someone's eye out, spend the rest of your life
under a pall. Granted, it must have been easy.

The similarities must have been monstrous then,
yet the obtuse angle of evening is mum on the subject.

Tower of Darkness

I cannot remain outside any longer
in the cold and pervasive rain.
I grab my crotch wishing for a ball of light
in the shaggy interior other people have.
I shall go away without fetching a grain
from the earth,
              compact,
                        with the climbing design
we knew and hated so well, and when it was our turn
to die we just gave up, mumbling some excuse.

Do you often go to see them?
They can't have much cause
to journey here, yet their footprints,
foreclosed by snow . . .

It was the barker whose patter started it
well before we were awake, into the dawn
that grizzles, now, a fright
                    to be wished, to be read,
unlike the old healing that will come again in time.

Tremendous Outpouring

According to most of these people, a good "ladle"
is hard to get—mothers of such things, the cousins, added on,
splashing and crying. I brushed him. Let others watch
the espaliered proof, the tapered belfry. The human gust.

Little things like that—would I
like to request it? No.
In the cold night, spun out of the past,
the names. Frost. An obscure petulance fattens the rafters
overhead, bulges the curtains. The cigarette boat
goes out. The urban brewery
coincided with the jingle in my pants
to chill those ways.

Tuesday Evening

She plundered the fun in his hair.
The others were let go.
There was a wet star on the stair.
Upstairs it had decided to snow.

Not everyone gets off at this stop
the turtlelike conductor said.
If you'd like to hear those beans hop
it could be arranged in your head.

Now from every side, cheerleaders
and their disc-eyed boyfriends come.
The latter put up bird feeders.
Birds alight on them and are dumb

with anticipation of the meal.
The punishment is not due
in our time said the wise old eel.
Its overture is still distant in the blue

sign of a vacant factory. You'll know
when it starts up. Darn! That's what I thought
it would be, I said. Isn't there a hoe
somewhere to root these weeds out?

Or a chair on a blanket
of a manor house in time
and shouldn't we somehow thank it
for the perfection of the climb?

Straight over roads, in culottes
the marching women go. Why besmirch
that casket, choose fleshpots
over a stand of young birch?

The veranda failed to make an impression,
ditto the lavaliere.
Potted ferns have become my obsession,
waltzing under the chandelier.

No one weeps to me anymore.
Then up and spake greengrocer Fred:
"Time and love are a whore
and after the news there is bed

to take to. Don't you agree?
It's lonely to believe, but it's half
the fun. Here, take a pee
on me, but over there by that calf."

The things we thought of naming
are crystals now. You can see from the porte cochere
now a small business flaming,
now the besotted rind of some pear.

It all seems ages ago—that time
of not being able to choose
or think of a rhyme
for "so many books to peruse

until the body is done." A chicken
might pass by and never notice
us standing pale as a mannequin,
clutching a fistful of myosotis

as though this would matter some day to some lover
when the time was ripe and our mooring
had been sliced. Then it would be time to rediscover
a plashing that would seem more alluring

for being ancient. You see, the past
never happened. Nothing can survive long in its heady
embrace. Our memories are a simulcast
of lost conventions, already

drowning in their sleep. In some such
wise we outgrew ourselves, lianas
over lichen. Forasmuch
as sweetness comes to the nicotianas

only at evening, your arrangement is overbred,
threadbare. You may want to think about this
a little. Down in their pavilion, whose overfed
airs waft lightly, naughtily, Dad and Sis

are waving, calling your name, over
and over again. But it's like a wall of veil
tipped in. We can dance only alone. Rover
senses an advantage—it's the Airedale

from the next block again. To keep even the peace
sounds extraneous, now. How many senses
do we need? Our motives predecease
our cashing them in. Fences

will be happy to relieve you of that icon
for a small consideration. And you,
what about you? Slowly unraveling, the chaconne
sizes us up: right pew,

wrong church. O if ever the devil
comes to claim his due, let it be after
the touching ceremony, yet before the revel
becomes frenzied, and ambitions turn to laughter.

Resist, friends, that last day's dying.
The melodious mode obtains. Always
remember that. At trying
moments, practice the art of paraphrase.

Just because someone hands you something of value
don't imagine you're in it for the money.
You can always tell a gal-pal you
prefer the snakeroot's scented hegemony.

Or go for a walk. It counts too.
In my charming madness I dress plainer
than when they used to mispronounce you,
but what's correct streetwear in N'Djamena

clashes in the old upstate classroom.
Come, we're weak enough to share a posset,
divide with the boys another hecatomb.
All other rodomontades are strictly bullshit.

Such are the passwords that tired Aeneas
wept for outside the potting shed,
when, face pressed to the pane, he sought Linnaeus'
sage advice. And the farm turned over a new leaf instead.

We can't resist; we're all thumbs, it seems,
when it comes to grasping mantras.
The oxen are waiting for us downstream; academe's
no place for botanizing; the tantra's

closed to us. Song and voice, piano and flowers,
abduct us to their plateau.
Look—becalmed, a horse devours
buttercups in the ruts by an old château.

If this is about being regal, it must be Japan
has assented. Let's take the vaporetto
to where it goes. A sea cucumber of marzipan
promises decorum. The boatman quaffs Amaretto.

Well, and this is the way I've always done it. A fricative
voice from this valley wants to think so. Those jars of ointment
are still untouched. Were patients always so uncommunicative?
Even Jeremy? He's late for his appointment,

and I must go down an inclined plane
to the city's anthill, with only dissolved rage
for company. And should some perdurable chatelaine
gain control over the police, must we summon the archimage

to bandage the hurt? Only a little moisture
remains at the tip of the tongue, a pro forma
signal of engagement. Before the great rupture,
still a duo, we sang the "Casta Diva" from *Norma*

on Sunday morning. Now all's retrograde;
the new openness cloys. Pencils are to sharpen,
yet I keep mine dull. My cockade
is tarnished, my dress puny, my shoes of cordovan

behind the bed. Sometimes I like to ride in a carriage,
over dales and downs. My fiancée is a lacrosse player.
When the moon is full one's in the mood for marriage,
amiable for a while. But the village soothsayer

warned us against it, of dreary days to come
unless we interacted on a vast scale. And who can predict
furtive new developments? Because we'd swum
the Hellespont long ago, in our youth, we assumed the verdict

would be sealed by now. And you know, only anonymous
lovers seem to make it to the altar. The rest are branded
with a time and place, and rarely know each other. The eponymous
host of the Bridge and Barrel, a moralist, was openhanded,

yet nothing could bar the tear from one blue eye. He'd chattered
vainly till now. So I assumed the aggressor's fate.
Behind the door crockery clattered
mysteriously, the beadle was stunned, the boilerplate

contract wilted in the intense heat
of the deluged afternoon. Even when the tumbrel
arrived, it seemed it would have to wait
for the century to catch up. Meanwhile, in the adumbral

hall not a whistle could be heard, no screams, no catcalls,
unless you counted the willows' sobbing.
Evening came on boisterous. Pirouettes and pratfalls
were executed before an admiring crowd. Demons were hobnobbing

with whatever entered on skis. To have proffered
only this was sublimely sufficient. But what of cattails
loosing seeds on the air like milkweed? A scoffer'd
not turn away, just this once, for what prevails

is most certainly what will be current
years from now: celadon pods with opal juices
oozing from them. Fruits of the sand, blackcurrant
and bayberry, and a crowd of mild smiles, a burnoose's

wandering cord. When needed to combat flatulence,
the correct pills turn up in pairs. I mistook embroidery
in the stair carpet for something else, the doll's petulance
for a sign from the heavens. The whole darn menagerie

is after me now; I have strength for but one curtain call,
and that a swift one. But will the critics
recite my reasons? Luckily a landfall
materialized in the nick of time. Luckily my desire wasn't great. Politics

overwhelms us all. In seasons of strife we compose palinodes
against the breakers, retracting what was lithe
in our believing. By evening, its heresy implodes
under an August moon; repercussions writhe

in a context of mangroves. Perfervid scroungers
invade the Catalog Fulfillment Center, diverting the sick energy
in our wake into easeful light, and day. A few loungers
on the mezzanine are puzzled, but most are not. The ambient lethargy

incises its monogram on the walls of bathhouses, in wooden
tunnels: To wit, man plays a role in his conspiracy,
ergo, he cannot be a victim. After a sudden
denouement, the climate again turns bland; its apostasy

was too minute to register on God's barometer.
Only an occasional letter to the *Times*
hinted that a change might have occurred.
Otherwise it was *beau fixe* on the speedometer

as it raced toward clayey lands with windmills
and similar giddy appurtenances. From far,
from night and morning, innovations arrive in schools, whippoorwills
are calling. The Circolo Italiano welcomes new adherents, a streetcar

bearing members of the Supreme Court floats in the sky like a zeppelin.
It was all over in a trance. Now it's the fiction
weighs us down, an iron corset. Adrenaline
is channeled into new, virtuoso ways, wherein constriction

is viewed as normal, soothing as an antimacassar.
Better to live in a fictive aura, I say, than putter
in one's garden forever, praying to NASA
at dusk, as in Millet's *Angelus*, closing a shutter

on substantive dreaming. That, after all, is where we're
at. It is time for the rebuilding of melody
on a grand scale. Reread Shakespeare; a fakir here
and there won't sabotage the kernel of parody

baked into the airiest ontological *mille feuilles*, nor change that gold
back into straw. The medicine men knew what they were doing when
they lanced boils with direct imaging. Charm gained a foothold,
then exploded into bronze deities. No matter, the regimen

practiced by the ancients, i.e., inhaling
dust and air near a body of water, is still around to restore
lost fossils of wit to their living, vibrant selves, unveiling
a menu both familiar and alluring. Before

quitting this backdrop of a Renaissance piazza, open
your body and mind to all comers. They are both factory and garden
to the happy few, thunderstorms to some, a dull weapon
though fierce, to others. And as attitudes harden,

the lost light stares as a man in pajamas
crosses the ravaged street. All this decision-making entails
sophomoric stunts and impatience. From the Bahamas
to Torquay stretches the dun pilgrimage. Cocktails

infiltrate it, but the man knows he must go
just so far and stop, that his beloved will have forgotten
him by then. He must choose the stars or the snow,
a naked stick figure. All the rotten

things that can befall a man with a comb and toothbrush
already happened to him, leagues ago. And there is no ending
it. Yet the past is profitless slush,
same as the present. Tomorrow is on hold, pending,

and great lizards infiltrate the Dalmatian-spotted
sky. Was it for this you gave yourself up
to some cause or other, that has now trickled away, dotted
with colored pom-poms? Only a final hiccup

sits on the step, awaiting orders. You were wrong about language,
see. Its arrows are raining down like ejected porcupine
quills. An archer (Robin Hood, for instance) could gauge
the correct distance between identical hummocks. Which is fine

with me, except I don't think anybody's going to notice
the directive that brought you here. Best to marshal the
secondary promptings and forget the awful journey before rigor mortis
sets in. You mean it hasn't? Right. Then I'm still in the Marshalsea,

my dependency shall never cease! And there's a kind of happiness,
though a bitter one, in that. I'm going to cash in my chips
and quit while I'm winning. The loveliness
of statues of statesmen survives, a barcarole drips

from their sagging jaws, graphic as springtime.
In twos and threes, peasants
vanish behind yon ridge. The celestial pantomime
engulfs them slowly. The pheasants

of our kingdom aren't as plump as yours. No matter.
I'll wager a microclimate's responsible. And did your sister
ever loan you those three bucks? No, the regatta
closed down while we were still ogling its pinnaces, and a twister

slashed through at that precise moment, there was nowhere
to hide, in the confusion we got separated.
Now I must arise and go where
the flying fishes play, and poppies perplex the cultivated

plain. Go ahead, I'll keep an eye on things, you can breathe
easy. It's what I had in mind: a sail printed all over
with musical staves. I would unsheathe
love's whippet and embrace us all, even if Rover

never growled again. "Springs, when they happen, happen elsewhere.
A certain sexiness . . ." ventured the prince. But where, oh where, is
    the nectar
that makes babes of us? Our printout's in disrepair,
the parterres are fading, and the projector

is spinning out of control. Half a hundred youths
could sustain us, swimming in the moat
with reeds to breathe through. The emptied booths
by the front gate are cheerless indeed. A stoat

swept by me on the waters, halfway to refurbished oblivion,
but my antennae suggest nothing apposite
to formalize his trajectory. A safe-conduct from the Bolivian
chargé d'affaires flutters in the breeze of my room. In the windows
    opposite,

a massacre is reflected. Is it meant as codicil,
or mere free-form tangling? Anyway, night is serendipitous
again; swallows clutter my windowsill;
bats are executing stately arabesques. A precipitous

slide into belief must have occurred recently, but left no earnest
of its passing. A videotape of sports bloopers
keeps unreeling, determined to rescue its syllabus from the furnace
of eternity; airheads are treated roughly. One of those Victorian
    peasoupers

is equalizing everything, titmouse and pterodactyl
alike. When it will be the fashion again we'll have trochees
galore. Even the bellicose double-dactyl
will flourish for a time, in Okefenokees

of subjectivity. Lakes will overflow, bargain
counters shrivel to nothing, the Great Bear look away, brittle
talismans explode at dormer windows. The degradation Ruskin
warned against is back, a heap of frozen spittle.

We see one thing next to another. In time they get superimposed
and then who looks silly? Not us, as you might think, but the curve
we are plotted on, head to head, a parabola in the throes
of vomiting its formula, piqued by the sullen verve

of day, while night is siphoned off again. And as wolverines
prefer Michigan, so this civil branch of holly is nailed to your door,
      lest you
fear my coming, or any uncivil declaiming, or submarines
in the bay that spreads out before us, or any gumshoe.

We'll party when the millennium gets closer. Meanwhile
I wanted to mention your feet. A dowser
could locate your contentedness zone. But where have you been while
folk dancing broke out, and colorful piñatas, waking Bowser

in his kennel, rendering the last victuals
in the larder unappetizing? Yet those feet shall impose the glory
of my slogans on the unsuspecting world that belittles
them now, but shall whistle them *con amore*

anon. That doesn't mean "peace at any price,"
but a shaking-down of old, purblind principles
that were always getting in the way. Self-sacrifice
will be on the agenda, a lowering of expectations, a ban on municipal

iron fences and picnics. Man must return to his earth,
experience its seasons, frosts, its labyrinthine
processes, the spectacle of continual rebirth
in one's own time. Only then will the sunshine

each weekday lodges in its quiver expand till the vernal
equinox rounds it off, then subtracts a little more each day,
though always leaving a little, even in hyperboreal climes where eternal
ice floes fringe the latitudes. On a beautiful day in May

you might forget this, but there it is, always creeping up on you.
Permit me then for the umpteenth time to reiterate
that basking in the sun like an otter or curlew
isn't the whole story. Tomorrow may obliterate

your projects and belongings, casting a shadow longer than the equator
into your private sector, to wit, your plan to take a Hovercraft
across the lagoon and have lunch there, leaving the waiter
a handsome tip. For though your garrison be fully staffed,

the near future, like an overcrowded howdah,
trumpets its imminent arrival, opens the floodgate
of a thousand teeming minor ills, spoiling the chowder
and marching society's annual gymkhana, letting in smog to asphyxiate

palms and eucalpytuses. One paddles in the backwash of the present,
laughing at its doodles, unpinning its robes,
smoothing its ribbons, and lo and behold an unpleasant
emu is blocking the path; its one good eye probes

your premises and tacit understandings, and the outing
is postponed till another day. Or you could be reclining
on a rock, like Fra Diavolo, and have it sneak up on you, spouting
praise for the way the city looks after a shower, divining

its outer shallows from the number of storm windows
taken down and stashed away, for it has the shape of a sonata—
bent, unyielding. And, once it's laid out in windrows,
open to the difficult past, that of a fish on a platter.

Expect no malice from it and freshets
will foam, gathering strength as they leapfrog the mountain.
But a quieter realism plumbs the essence of ponds, as nitwits
worship the machine-tooled elegies of the fountain,

that wets its basin and the nearby grass. In a moment the dustmen
will be here, and in the time remaining it behooves
me to insist again on the lust men
invent, then cherish. But since my mistress disapproves,

I'll toe the line. And should you ask me why, sir,
I'll say it's because one's sex drives are like compulsive handwashing:
better early on in life than late. Yet I'm still spry, sir,
though perhaps no longer as dashing

as in times gone by, and can wolf down the elemental
in one gulp—its "How different one feels after doing something:
calm, and in a calm way almost tragic; in any case far from the
    unwholesome
figure we cut in the reveries of others, a rum thing

not fit to be seen in public with." Yet it is this ominous bedouin
whose contours blur us when someone glimpses
us, and is what we are remembered as, for no one can see our genuine
side falling to pieces all down our declamatory gestures. They treat
    pimps as

equals, ignoring all shortcomings save ours. And of course, no commerce
is possible between these two noncommunicating vessels of our being.
As urushiol
is to poison ivy, so is our own positive self-image the obverse
of all that will ever be said and thought about us, the vitriol

we gargle with in the morning, just as others do. This impasse
does, however, have an escape clause written into it: planned
enhancements, they call it. So that if one *is* knocked flat on his ass
by vile opprobrium, he need only consult his pocket mirror: The sand

will seem to flow upward through the hourglass; one is pickled
in one's own humors, yet the dismantled ideal
rescued from youth is still pulsing, viable, having trickled
from the retort of self-consciousness into the frosted vial

of everyone's individual consciousness noting it's the same
as all the others, with one vital difference: It belongs to no one.
Thus a few may climb several steps above the crowd, achieve fame
and personal fulfillment in a flaring instant, sing songs to one

more beloved than the rest, yet still cherish the charm and quirkiness
that entangle all individuals in the racemes
of an ever-expanding Sargasso Sea whose murkiness
comes at last to seem exemplary. So, between two extremes

hidden in blue distance, the dimensionless
regions of the self do have their day. We like this, that,
and the other; have our doubts about certain things; enjoy pretension
less
than we did when we were young; are not above throwing out a caveat

or two; and in a word are comfortable in the saddle
reality offers to each of her children, simultaneously
convincing each of us we're superior, that no one else could straddle
her mount as elegantly as we. And when, all extraneously,

the truth erupts, and we find we are but one of an army of
    supernumeraries
raising spears to salute the final duet
between our ego and the endlessly branching itineraries
of our *semblables*, a robed celebrant is already lifting the cruet

of salve to anoint the whole syndrome. And it's their proper
perspective that finally gets clamped onto things and us, including
our attitudes, hopes, half-baked ambitions, psychoses: everything an
    eavesdropper
already knows about us, along with the clothes we wear and the
    brooding

interiors we inhabit. It's getting late; the pageant
oozes forward, act four is yet to come, and so is dusk.
Still, ripeness must soon be intuited; a coolant
freeze the tragic act under construction. Let's husk

the ear of its plenitude, forget additional worries,
let Mom and apple pie go down the tubes, if indeed
that's their resolve. For, satisfying as it is to fling a pot, once the slurry's
reached the proper consistency, better still is it to join the stampede

away from it once it's finished. Which, as of now,
it is. Wait a minute! You told us eternal flux
was the ordering principle here, and in the next breath you disavow
open-endedness. What kind of clucks

153

do you take us for, anyway? Everyone knows that once something's
    finished,
decay sets in. But we were going to outwit all that. So
where's your panacea now? The snake oil? Smoke and mirrors?
    Diminished
expectations can never supplant the still-moist, half-hesitant tableau

we thought to be included in, and to pursue
our private interests and destinies in, till doomsday. Well, I
never said my system was foolproof. You did too! I did not. Did too!
Did not. Did too. Did not. Did too. Hell, I

only said let's wait awhile and see what happens, maybe
something will, and if it doesn't, well, our personal
investment in the thing hasn't been that enormous, you crybaby;
we can still emerge unscathed. These are exceptional

times, after all. And all along I thought I was pointed
in the right direction, that if I just kept my seat
I'd get to a destination. I knew the instructions were disjointed,
garbled, but imagined we'd eventually make up the lost time. Yet one
    deadbeat

can pollute a whole universe. The sensuous green mounds
I'd been anticipating are nowhere to be seen. Instead, a dull
urban waste reveals itself, vistas of broken masonry, out of bounds
to the ordinary time traveler. How, then, did he lull

us, me and the others, into signing on for the trip?
By exposing himself, and pretending

not to see. Solar wind sandpapers the airstrip,
while only a few hundred yards away, bending

hostesses coddle stranded voyagers with canapés
and rum punch. To have had this in the early stage,
not the earliest, but the one right after the days
began to shorten imperceptibly! And one's rage

was a good thing, good for oneself and even
for others, at that critical juncture. Dryness
of the mouth was seldom a problem. Winking asides would leaven
the dullest textbook. Your highness

knows all this, yet if she will but indulge
my wobbling fancies a bit longer, I'll . . . Where was I? Oh, and then
a great hurricane came, and took away the leaves. The bulge
in the calceolaria bush was gone. By all the gods, when

next I saw him, he was gay, gay as any jackanapes. Is
this really what you had in mind, I asked.
But he merely smiled and replied, "None of your biz,"
and walked out onto the little peninsula and basked

as though he meant it. And in a funny kind of way, the nifty
feeling of those years has returned. I can't explain it,
but perhaps it means that once you're over fifty
you're rid of a lot of decibels. You've got a tiger; so unchain it

and then see what explanations they give. Walk through
your foot to the place behind it, the air

will frizz your whiskers. You're still young enough to talk through
the night, among friends, the way you used to do somewhere.

An alphabet is forming words. We who watch them
never imagine pronouncing them, and another opportunity
is missed. You must be awake to snatch them—
them, and the scent they give off with impunity.

We all tagged along, and in the end there was nothing
to see—nothing and a lot. A lot in terms of contour, texture,
world. That sort of thing. The real fun and its clothing.
You can forget that. Next, you're

planning a brief trip. Perhaps a visit to Paul Bunyan
and Babe, the blue ox. There's time now. Piranhas
dream, at peace with themselves and with the floating world. A grunion
slips nervously past. The heat, the stillness are oppressive.
     Iguanas . . .

Twilight Park

Surely the lodger hadn't returned yet.
He had, but she hadn't heard him.
He was waiting five steps below the landing:
a black cloth in one black-gloved hand,
a band of light from the streetlamp like masking tape
across his eyes. He wanted to write something that would *sell*,
and this seemed the only way.
                    Desperate are the remedies
when one is broke, and no longer all that young or handsome.

Attention, secondary characters, and that means you,
Edith Fernandez: The snow is no longer pallid enough
to sum up your footfalls. One is ever so impatient;
now the tape falls, now carnival music
bashes in the front door. One can never be wholly
right, or wrong: catsup or ketchup? We must reread this.
The ending is considered particularly fine.

Umpteen

In this childhood you can
sort of tell by manners, like tomatoes,
who looked to be—may be—

like cute monsters who don't go away
but are never any trouble,
but what's *behind* it, this anything?

Is anything behind what we say
when we are not alone, not too far apart,
otherwise constricted?

Like a novel read on shipboard
or an old play with complicated stage directions
that may never have been carried out.

Perhaps the snow scene was too difficult,
the bison stampede too compromising.
We wake and are physical, the morning and

a thousand nerve endings are chiding,
clamoring . . . and all for what?
These files have nothing on you.

What the Plants Say

Don't cry it's lentil soup!
Kind doll rush us away
to a situation where the hay is mortgaged.
It was in fact time for a roll in the hay
so beautifully reflected in the color Polaroid
in the estate agent's window, but it
wasn't time to go. And she channels us
out over the silver plain's mush—
no wonder everybody wanted Karelia,
chiggers and all, and then it *was*
time, time for dusk.

If only one outrageous jeweler thought it
why then it must be true. A Cadillac
with a platinum pretzel hood ornament—
why not! You and all
you're taking me to must be true,
and silent, bodacious. That's the way
I like 'em—mystery girls
with buttermilk braids and a microchip of plain
caring, over the deserted wall.
So much rubbish! or trash . . .

Well, the bird flew down the well
and that was the last ointment anyone wanted.
For sure we got to go. Now's
the time, Ida.

When All Her Neighbors Came

the most beautiful combination appeared
on the game board. Normally we don't do these things
to each other. There's always a little kissing,
ha ha. Of that you may be sure. Yes, but mostly
they don't go round together, tethered to a median
that takes itself for the Judgment. Well I can't be
picking apples and playing the piano simultaneously,
now, can I? A withered little bird applauds. Some day,
it says, you may go back to the glasshouse and fiddle
what we all were taught, from day one. Your ale-colored
shirt is only an onus. Inside the others are dry.

The "give and take" of the other schools
isn't what I had in mind, thank you. A snake,
perfect in its horror, is. And the bondsmen drift off,
the decision buried in papers for a century or two,
and we, why then we are too, frugal of spirit,
reacting to the latest news. This lady of costmary
is the essential spoon. We may live more patently,
more expectantly, now.

Where It Was Decided We Should Be Taken

Your name here invisible as a headache
starts it off again and we are rolling
helplessly between the trees—we should
have seen it coming, but not many
are able to do just that. So we
dusted off our knees it was nice
to hear from you again over so many moons
with stars in them and now it has
become time for you to become comfortable again
which is not romantic as hydrangeas
aren't romantic until you imagine
a shed for them to be in
to be in the darkness like lilies, overspending
their light it seems, always on the carpet
for something, on the incoming tide
that many faces surround.
                              Say it was
in some burrow you could hear planes overhead
but nothing was nasty this time, everybody
wanted to contribute to a general effort
which was being made

by a general on the other side of Kit Carson country.
Did I tell you about my hobby? It's—
Well, we can talk about my dreams if you wish.
I had a good one the other night
when everything was still
and in the morning I awoke with a red nightcap
on, really a dunce cap, of which
no one has ever seen one. I have a friend who

wants to collect them for a certain room in a
castle. But he can't.
There aren't any.

Another day I was out with Miss Peevish
paying calls, it seems like nobody's home anymore
and you have to walk so far to leave a card
over a stile and then a frog's in the
middle of the path—"Confrontational,"
she murmured. If only they asked *one*.
Cakes are optional, and credit.
They moved closer toward the sphere
of the lighthouse, the overcoat slid off,
revealing—in some way the boy gets in the way
all the time. Reason and habit
have beaten a path he's always circumnavigating,
but *this*! No one would ever—

These accents let us down
gently onto the torso of a wood
where birdcatchers yodel and bobwhites cheep.
It's not going very far, it's like going to the door
after the salesmen have slid into the universal pit.
And when one goes out it's time to go too,
as though Mother and the piano had never exited
and those china knobs you never put away.
Feed the horse on brambles the moon
is coming

Woman Leaning

However it may come back to you
it'll seem all right. At first.
Till the ones who do the realizing
realize, and call you to their office
at one in the morning.

I said fix the radiator.
These gray grapes are spread out before us
in a feast situation. Yet who can explain
why we should banquet here?

Then, in she plops—
a soloist trained to lead us
out of the briar patch of history,
trap that was always here.
And we, we listen. That's obvious.
There was more said in the tent,
but what I remember only has to do with paddling.
Then, inexplicably, we're safe.

No one loves us for it, yet
they can dictate to us now
from a striped sofa that was years in the making.
And what they tell us to write makes no difference
but is enough light for us to see by.
Everyone jumped over the fence safely.

All that was left was a book under a weeping
willow, in whose table of contents the glottal insistence
of the stream was repeated endlessly, like tears
for our benefit, if we should ever get to know them.

Yes, Dr. Grenzmer. How May I
Be of Assistance to You? What!
You Say the Patient Has Escaped?

We were staying at the Golden Something-or-Other.
Anyway, what does it matter now?
The boats have rolled up their colored sails.
The city is like a hinge. In the morning its glass
girders are flushed with light that gets drained
in the afternoon, but then something funny happens:
The westward-looking buildings reflect the sun's
rays more fiercely than they are projected.
They become a rival sunset in the east. That's heresy,
or at any rate bigamy. Tall buildings
"to suckle fools and chronicle small beer"; such is my story,
but I'm glad to be having this chance to tell it to you
even though we are in a silent movie and can speak only words
painted with milk. Yet someone comes to care about them:
There is always someone to care, somewhere,

but the sheriff vandalizes the day they return.
I didn't let you dream about it.
It is for this I am being punished
by reforms harder than the ones in Congress.
They have rules to go by, sins to atone for:
I, I have only weightlessness
and a vague feeling that I should be spending my time
doing other things—sweeping the apartment,
washing out a child's mouth with soap.

It was nugatory. They fed us delicacies
while we waited for the order of quilts to arrive—

or was it kilts? Joshua had this haunted feeling
he'd never finalized it at the start, when all
should have been beginning, but instead was pleased to slosh around
in mid-harbor. Anyway, there *were* invoices. Of that
he was almost certain. And a number of young girls
came and stood around the tree in which he was sitting—
were *they* the ones who had placed orders for the kilts?
Or were they mere raisin fanciers? "You'll see
when the weather gets dry and yellow the raisins
will form all by themselves, alone on the branches,
and no one will care. And those that like to eat them
real fast out of boxes won't have a clue
as to why that old horse-collar is draped over a branch
of the weeping willow, causing it to weep (that is,
bestir its leaves) even harder. Some people somewhere are prepared
for a few things to happen, but that's not counting us or our
immediate families. An apple-green boxcar slithers along
a distant railway, yearning for something
unnameable at the end of the canyon. Not
a handful of raisins, probably, but you catch my drift."

Soon all was drift. They had a feeling
they had better go inside, yet none could make a move
in that direction. All remained transfixed. "Tell them,"
the skald continued, "but only if they ask,
how this situation came about. We'll see then
what jury will convict me, just because I feel like a woman
trapped in a man's body, but only a little—not enough
to want to wear a skirt, but enough
to make me feel like putting on a kilt, and even then

only in Scotland, if I should be so lucky
as to find myself there some day." Tremors
stirred the little band; there was obvious sympathy
for his plight, mingled with something more acidulous,
like pickling spices. And all the girls turned away
to weep, but were changed to ivy
and stuff like that. Why am I telling you this?
To assuage my conscience, perhaps, hoping the bad dreams
will go away, or at least become more liberally mixed
with the good, for none are totally good
or bad, just like the people who keep walking into them,
and the scenery, familiar or obvious though it be.

Besides, I've raised one major issue—
at least credit me with that. It will be a long time
before this turns to nothing, and in the meantime
we can sit upon the ground, and tell sad stories
of the lives of pets, as the ground freezes and thaws
many times—it is past caring. And what goes on within us
will be inscribed by the dancing needle on our chart,
for others to consult and be derived from.
I thought it would all end casually on a bank
of flowers, but alas, a real bank was growing out of it
with tellers and guards. Who liked the flowers.

Yesterday, for Instance

No longer available is the hare
with milky fur grazing on the clover of memory.
O beautiful basketballs! How far stretch the docks,
farther than my bonny sailor is from me.

The pigeons shift. The sky is syrup and pink gold.
I can no longer lie. I must tell it "like it is."
But where is the raincoat that will hustle me
to the forest crossing? For it is a convenience

to know and to learn, and haply no good is in me.
I must claw the ground for grace. These poor root-systems
are in faith no better. I must see about clobbering
the backstairs monster on his toes, let him cover

my rail of defense with dandelion slips. Then I'll be off
into who knows whose trouble that the boarded-up sign
couldn't spell. And then after years and years
I'm back—but it's like two seconds on a conductor's watch.

He patronized me, and all I could say was, "Wow,
this is goofy!" And he liked me in it, with the croquet tresses.
And the buccaneer said it was too soon,
that we'd find out in the grass trap, which is why

I echoed. Even children couldn't pay attention
to all of it, and all of it is most certainly
where we are. No more candied lies. I'll come out as the movie
trailer ends. I promise the sun was a switch, or tickler.

You Dropped Something

So what if it's brackish my love
today's junk mail is full of arms for you
the erotic weavings of slumlord
hermits and piss-elegant diatribes:
No more waving for you
at least for the time being
which is anybody's stable

The lost nights thatched with regrets
shingled with antinomian heresy and hedged
about with ifs ands and buts
are nobody's dream cycle to you
the arena of matches and pups

and further slide
into romantic chaos
Say they're not keeping track anymore
that the wounded demoiselle is hopping
mad and more coal barges
have arrived on the harbor's
slippery surface

Say then that they're not well again
Jumping through hoops to train
myself to attract attention was always
sometimes my endeavor to attract
smart eyes

You that go out and go in
through memory's many castles

are you single or just alone this evening
castrati belch forth some
air thought to be unfit
for today's goads and geodes

She'll be coming round the house
and faster too; some press goodies
overlooked in the mad rush to prepubescent freedom
whose minds got mismatched

Throw many more daggers at the stone
It's ancient after all
how many comic strips do you invoke
what tarheels
in fashionable disarray
more strokes this morning

You come to the end of the row
you could switch over or begin a new one
at the wrong end and work back to the previous beginning
Do we really want to see it turn out all right
Are the guns trained on her
quarterdeck what about the ketch

And you do really go in

It's a passably elegant solution
for what was only land office before
ancient miles of wind picking
the harrow clean

All standing around
just to welcome you
you and your pie-eyed souvenir chest
and the bride you brought from back east
nailed to the sun

You, My Academy

Maybe untwine my breath, like.
Remove the cast-off castanets from my chest hair.
That's better. I can see more in the distance.
I won't be giving this up any time soon,

yet commerce no longer functions the way it used to
in the days gone by. Small businesses
are beginning to go the way of the peacherino,
following the Pied Piper and his rats
into the cavity beneath the hill. Even big business
is foreign to itself, knows not what it dreams,
or wants. If it glances into the mirror
at times, it sees only a blank, supplemental wall.
Profit-taking is an unheard-of concept.

Only muddled enjoyment perceives that a crossover
took place in the recent past. Huddled shapes
of the homeless, hidden under dirty quilts,
are the one sign of that baleful trajectory
that left the street full of cannonballs like horse manure.
Enjoyment becomes a rare earth amid such strata,
something the landlady was going to tell you
but you were too quick for her on the landing.
It's diffused now in the racing forms.

Fiona and Ilona, just back from Riga,
can't understand what's the fuss. "Weren't there
seventeen-story G-men back when, too? Anyway, the kids
haven't turned litmus pink—*or have they*?
What manner of golfer stands to reap anything

from this desperate situation?"
Ask a situationist, lady, I'm here for the free canapés
and the gin.

Bituminous ballocks thrash the sand spread outside.
It were time for the library, and to ferret out
who killed the sexton. "Not I," says the dung beetle,
"Nor I," the worm. But one of you surprised him in
the few seconds he went to get his pants. And my theory
is all but erected—an imposing pyramid
of squashes, eggplants, artichokes, leeks, celery, et al.
Is it too late to absorb that?

That's why screeds were written—for dictionaries
to read them, and then come to conclusions
that would have been startling once, maybe thirty-five years ago,
but now no longer have power to shock, or even charm
as butterflies laughed to us in childhood,
and the creamy sails on the marsh filled with the light and the wind.

It must be light and bright as a brazier
down where you are now. Are you going to fax us any fun?
I was just sitting on the toilet, dreaming a ruse
to make you factions obey, and here you ring my doorbell
and hand me a large box wrapped like a harlequin—
Is it full of dishes? Are you going to be my "wee one"
once the attorneys have sailed back?

Or do we lose each other in the desolate glens
it seems the world is largely composed of?
Is that where your pointed toe is leading?

I'd jump off buildings for you, scale circus tents,
though I know it's not exactly what you had in mind.
How about suburbia? "A sad pavane
for these distracted times." How about the Everglades,
then? A mangrove is a wondrous thing
that never stops growing, unlike
our pencil-thin projects for reaping dividends
once the troglodytes have had their way with us,
and been assimilated by us. That won't be for centuries,
but time's caprice is a wild card, compressing lives
into a space of weeks or months, if need be,
sometimes.
    And sometimes
when my horse looks at me, it's a great treat,
or a great fright. Animals are about the last to listen
as you read from the Book of Hours—they get frisky
with listening, and the natural beauty of everything
wants it so—cut up for lenses to devour,
or vague and transparent as a subpoena when a tractor
stops to give us a lift to the nearest menstruating sun.

You Would Have Thought

Meanwhile, back in
soulless America, people are having fun
as usual.

A bird visits a birdbath.
A young girl takes a refresher course
in polyhistory. My mega-units are straining
at the leash of spring.
The annual race is on—

white flowers in someone's hair.
He comes in waltzing on empty airs,

mulling the blue notes of your case.
The leash is elastic and receptive
but I fear I am too wrapped up in cloudlets
of my own making this time.

In the other time it was rain dripping
from a tree to a house to the ground—
each thing helping itself and another thing
along a little. That would be inconceivable
these days of receptive answers and aggressive querying.

The routine is all too familiar,

the stone path wearying.

———

Young People

Slowly he is eating the stars—
they are like the spines of books to him,
but don't throw two ladies or locations at him.

He called this Nomad's Land.
Yet it was clean and serious. Not, it is true,
cheerful. Not by any means. Yet the old men

in pajamas made a leisurely appearance.
Good times were on the phonograph.
Surely somebody can be his wife,

surely there are strong husbands for such women,
who keep a rifle in the broom closet
and never ask for i.d. Their colors:

those of a saffron strand at evening
in disappointed August. We rise with the swifts,
never to know what cut us loose.